CONTENTS

#BLACKOUT

REAL Issues and REAL Solutions to REAL Challenges
Facing Black Student Affairs Professionals

Edited by

Khristian Kemp-Delisser, Ed.D.

Quiana Stone

Joshua Fredenburg, Ed.D.

Nequel Burwell

INTRODUCTION

Black Student Affairs Professionals (BLKSAP) started in 2011 at the annual Great Lakes Association of College and University Housing Officers (GLACUHO) and at no point did we think that we would be where we are today. A group of graduate students and professionals sat around at a planned lunch at a TGI Fridays in Grand Rapids, MI, and we talked about what it meant to be Black in this field and some of our shared experiences. It was there that we came up with the idea of a hashtag that would show support and solidarity amongst professionals of color #blksap. A year later with encouragement from peers, the Facebook group was created. We did not think it would get much traction.

Over the years BLKSAP has grown. GLACUHO now holds an annual lunch and has inspired other affinity groups. We held our first BLKSAP meet up at The Placement Exchange (TPE) in 2012 during a lunch hour in Orlando, FL and had about 20 people attend. At that same conference, we held our first NASPA meetup in the main conference hotel lobby. Never in our wildest dreams did we believe a simple hashtag would turn into a community that supports over 11,000 Black student affairs professionals across the country. There was never a set goal on what we wanted to accomplish; we just wanted to be seen, heard, and supported.

For quite some time Black Student Affairs Professionals felt that a lot of problematic statements and postings were happening in various social media spaces that catered to Student Affairs Professionals. What were supposed to be spaces for collegiality, networking, and dialogue were becoming spaces where professionals of colors felt unwelcome. On Friday, March 25, 2016, a group of BLKSAP Facebook members Bulaong Ramiz, Brittany Nicole Horton, and Jonathan Paul organized a plan and BLKSAP served as a space of support. They wanted to make an impact and let our colleagues in the field and across the country know that we have voices that need to be heard, we have stories and experiences that have changed and challenged us over the years. They expressed the frustrations of microaggressions, racial battle fatigue, and the struggle of working with peers who were in the majority who just didn't get it. They wanted our non-people of color colleagues to hear us. So they orchestrated the #BLKSAPBLACKOUT that took over the Student Affairs Professionals page and inundated the group with stories, pictures, articles, and think pieces to show them that we have a place in this field, and we would no longer be kept silent, or continue to take the responsibility of educating people who had all the tools and resources to be proactive about educating themselves. From that experience, the idea to create a book to share those stories was birthed.

There have been several ups and downs as it has come to the completion of this books; lots of job/title/career changes. But it is all worth it to know the stories of colleagues, and other student affairs professionals would be shared. The #BLACKOUT was magical the response was unexpected but so needed. It wasn't just a social media impact, I know many of our campuses were also impacted by what members of our group did in such a positive way, so I thank those courageous members for using their voices. Being able to share those stories with you all will be long overdue and completely rewarding. We hope you enjoy the stories and these personal experiences that were shared from other members of the community who were impacted by the #Blackout experience.

Personal Experiences with #Blackout

As a Black Student Affairs Administrator, I face racism, microaggressions, sexism, and I am often shunned for my support of my students, family, and colleagues within the LGBTQIA+ community. I have also had to deal with administrators at my institution (in my PRESENCE) make disparaging comments about people from a lower SES. I came from a lower SES and quite frankly, as an educator, I'm still there. Sometimes my experience is no different than my students. My voice will not be erased.

#BLKSAP #Blackout

- Veratta Simone

Thank you to everyone who is participating in the Blackout movement this morning. As an aspiring student affairs professional it excites me to know there are so many of y'all who care about the inclusivity of their students of color. Thank you for making sure higher education is accessible and has a place for marginalized identities. Also, thank you for providing so many amazing resources for everyone to connect with and continue educating ourselves. Keep fighting the good fight. #Blackout

- Jose Jacob Arce

As an African American student in an IFC organization, It really upsets me when an older member of an NPHC organization sees my letters (ATΩ) and because I'm Black they automatically assume that my fraternity is an academic fraternity or I'm told "So you think you're too good for a Black fraternity?" What's wrong with wanting to be a member of an organization that shares my beliefs and values? #BlkSAP #blksaBlackout#Blackout

- Mike Harris

When you're supposed to be working but your eyes are glued to this #Blackout happening in the other group. So many great resources being shared! Thank you, colleagues.

- Tristen Brenaé Johnson

Been reading the post regarding #Blackout and I got to say it's powerful and informative. As a Black male beginning on this journey into a profession where many of our Black youth especially Black men are struggling. I feel it is my major duty and obligation to fight against all others who feel my voice in this field shouldn't be heard. Well, hell with that can't wait to fight to make sure our students get the proper treatment and resources available to them and to push forward... fight on!

- Sean Hembrick

One of the SAP Admins would like this to be known to the members of this group.... if you are experiencing a personal backlash due to the BLKSAP Blackout them let them know. Her exact words are as follows:

Absolutely. If you need a "statement" or anything that will help you in gathering your documentation of today, please let me know. It would be my pleasure and the very least I could do. Please, please let me know if ANYONE is causing problems for the movement! Yes! I just don't want silent attacks to be taking place. I want to help. - Alexandra Fields - reposted with permission

- Krystal Rawls

For those of you who seek change in the field of Higher Education please recognize that you are appreciated. As we know higher education was established for certain White males to prosper and that institutions such as HBCUs and PBCUs and predominantly Hispanic serving institutions were created to offer a space during s time were these populations could not attend PWIs. When hosting conversations on how as a White professional you can make spaces more welcoming not only for Black staff, faculty, and students but ALL students of color please make sure that they are sitting at the table so there is s full understanding of what is occurring and how you, how we all can be agents of change! #Blksap #Blackout

- Jammal Stroud

"If you have come to help me, you are wasting your time. If you have come because your liberation is bound up with mine, then let us work together." - Lilla Watson

Standing right alongside the #BLKSAP #Blackout as a member of the Latinx SA Pro community. And THANK YOU for today's post.

- Keith D. Garcia

Started as a result of racially painful conversations that consistently happen on this page. There was a discussion about BLKSAP collectively leaving this page as a result, however, we were encouraged by a fellow colleague that we need to be vocal and live and force our colleagues to learn, listen, and engage. So three colleagues organized this Black out for today as a method of sharing resources and challenging our White colleagues that often perpetuate the violence and oppression in this group. It should be noted that it started with Black women and QPOC.

- Jerad Green

To my BLKSAP FAM today you embodied what Black excellence truly is. I love you all for constantly challenging me, supporting me, and helping to mold me into the best possible person and professional I can be. Let's keep the momentum going! And with that, I bid you all a good night. #melanin #blksapBlackout

- Barbara Rose

Last one from me (for now...I think...not sure yet...)

We, BLKSAP, are professionals and got your attention today.

Now, take a moment and a deep breath, and think about all that transpired today in this group. Think about how this is probably the first time there have been so many SAPros of color active in this group.

This might be the first time you have experienced colleagues of color sharing, being vulnerable, speaking out, and standing up en masse.

Now, take ALL of those thoughts and turn them towards your students of color. Yes, #BLKSAPBlackout was partially about the SAPro group not being a safe, welcoming place for many us. But, #BLKSAPBlackout is also about students of color. Many of our campuses are true battlefields for our students. #BLKSAPBlackout is for them for we SAPros of color were, are, and forever will be them. Some of the things said in this group are truly hurtful, damaging, and trauma - inducing to us as professionals. If we are experiencing this from our colleagues, our professional peers for crying out loud, then what are students of color experiencing?

(Note before someone gets it twisted, that last question is rhetorical.)

- Maary Loouisee

#BLKSAP BLACKOUT reminds me of how taxing it is to do this very crucial work.

WON'T STOP.

#CHAMP #takescourage #saltlifeandlove

#BLKSAP #blksapBlackout

#feeling determined.

- LJ Burgess

Good Morning Colleagues,

On behalf of the admin team, I'd like to take a moment to issue a statement of support to our members participating in the #blksapBlackout action that is taking place today here in the Student Affairs Professional Facebook group.

As many of you have likely noticed, there has been an incredible, organized "takeover" of the group which has resulted in postings of content that speaks to concerns around White privilege, microaggressions, allyship, racism, etc. It is important that we share that we believe all of the content we've seen thus far is not only valuable but also directly related to the important work we do in Student Affairs and Higher Education.

None of the content we've seen posted has been abusive to anyone – it only highlights the abuse and challenges our colleagues who identify as People of Color experience every day. We are aware that these same individuals often face microaggressions and abuse in this very group, and although we are nowhere near perfect, we have made a commitment to be better in supporting ALL members of the group equitably.

If you are uncomfortable with the #blksapBlackout movement, we welcome you to turn off notifications for the group and/or remove yourself from the group. You have the privilege of ignoring these messages – while many of our colleagues do not have that same privilege in real life.

If you have any questions or concerns, please do not hesitate to reach out to the admin team.

In solidarity,

SAPro Facebook Admin Team
Alexandra Fields

#BLACKOUT

CHAPTER 1
Authenticity Challenges Within The Workplace For African American Student Affairs Professionals

When You Are Needed, But Not Wanted
Author: Patricia Tita Feraud-King

"Don't go for something that sounds sexy on paper," stated my professor as she poured my class a glass of her great wisdom at the end of the semester. Truer words never rang so clear and I wished I heeded her advice months prior. I thought I hit the gold mine when I found a high-paying graduate assistantship dedicated to social justice. Sadly, working there as a Black cisgender women was a great nightmare.

My first day should have set off an alarm: when I first walked in, I noticed that I was the only staff of color, besides the student staff. Perplexed because we were located in an urban neighborhood where we primarily served low-income people of color, I went home and talked to my partner about my first day at work. He rhetorically asked, "they must be aware that the diversity is bad because why else would they hire someone like you, knowing that you wear your identity on your sleeve, you have radical ideas, and your history of activism?" I agreed with him and reasoned with myself that the staff must be aware of their White privilege and want to strive to promote social justice.

Admittedly, I loved the work I did because I was able to challenge the status quo and provide a safe space for my students. The students were down-to-Earth, open-minded, and always willing to engage. I felt that I was fulfilling my vocation. Sadly this feeling did not mitigate the toxic environment, where staff members would take credit for the work that they collaborated with me on and even my individual work. Several times in meetings, I would have to correct people when they were praising other staff members for my work. On numerous occasions, I was tempted to not speak at our staff meetings, or to certain individuals because some of the staff members would distort and claim my ideas as their own.

The blood boiled in my skin as I sat in many workshops and discussions where the staff members talked about "social justice" and "White privilege". I challenged the staff members on ways they perpetuate the unjust system in their lives; their responses were half-hearted and empty. As other college campuses across the nation became vocal about racial injustice and awareness increased about Black bodies being brutalized by police, my staff colleagues thought it was appropriate to talk about the issues in a trivial manner. It was as if they were chatting about the weather. Many times I wanted to call out "Black" because I was experiencing racial trauma and had no outlet at work.

I felt voiceless and invisible. I cringe thinking back at the multiple conversations I had with various staff members, including my direct supervisor, on how "it felt like the full-time staff did not see me" and how I "contributed" to the team, but was not "part of" the team. As the sole graduate assistant, I may work really hard to be "part of the team" and be "connected", but the full-time staff had the ultimate power and privilege of including me. As the only person of color, who attended all their full-time staff weekly meetings and ran the most workshops and student meetings throughout the week, how could they not see me! It was especially demoralizing to hear my supervisor's solution was for me to make the effort to stop by every office to say hello, so the full-time staff can "see me". As a women of color, I worked hard to be seen and heard on a daily basis in an elitist environment.

Should I Stay...

Although my environment was toxic, I did not want to leave because I enjoyed the work and felt that I needed to practice what I preached. Social justice work requires one to challenge the status quo, especially those in power. I rationalized that there was always a con to everything, but it did not mean I should quit. My job needed me because who else was going to challenge these administrators on their privilege and their oblivious behaviors toward reinforcing unjust social relations. I served as a confidant for students, particularly the students of color. Since I was willing to stay and take on the challenge of pushing for a more inclusive environment, I developed several survival strategies over time. I had to tell myself:

"No, you are not delusional!" I had to remind myself that

the racial microaggressions I was feeling at work were real. Racial microaggression, coined by Chester Pierce in the 1970s, is "the brief and everyday slights, insults, indignities and denigrating messages sent to people of color by well-intentioned White people who are unaware of the hidden messages being communicated," (Sue, 2010).

Sometimes, it is hard for one to pinpoint exactly whether or not they are actually experiencing racial microaggression. It is pertinent to remember that the intentions of the offending person or group do not matter, so as long as they are marginalizing someone with their actions. As a guest speaker from my graduate assistantship once asserted, it is necessary for one's intention to align with their actions in order to produce positive results. If I felt uncomfortable based on the way I was treated at my graduate assistantship, nobody can tell me otherwise on the way I felt.

Don't let the oppressor keep you silent: I made it a point to not let the microaggressions keep me quiet; instead, I channeled that frustration and challenged the staff members in meetings and private discussions. Those times when I felt repressed, I asked myself, *"If I did not stay and say something, then who would"* I never wanted to look back and think *"Why did I not say anything?"* Most importantly, I did not want the staff members to think that I was okay with their behavior.

Recruit a support team (even if it is a team of two): Ideally, it would have been nice if I could have recruited a "support team" within my graduate assistantship because I would have someone "on my side" when I felt slighted. Fortunately for me, having a friend, who worked at graduate assistantship near me and was dealing with a similar issue was oddly comforting. Similar to the cliche, "misery loves company," I was glad that I was not the only one dealing with a horrible graduate assistantship because my friend could empathize with me and served as a rock.

'Seek professional help': There is a stigma in the Black community in regards to receiving mental health treatment (NAMI, n.d.). Growing up, I often heard "only White people go see therapists because they are the crazy ones." Even though I knew that therapy is like having a conversation with an unbiased friend who is trained to help one through their difficulties, I will admit that I unconsciously viewed therapy in a negative light. Research shows that racism, including microaggressions, can lead to psychological distress, especially in the Black community (Williams, 2015). I needed the help, but did not seek it.

Instead of going to therapy, I overwhelmed my partner with the emotional labor of dealing with my distress. My partner obviously wanted me to no longer feel upset and anxious about my situation, but my partner was not professionally trained to assist me; this caused problems in our relationship. Towards the end of the semester, I felt the stress was too much and finally sought out professional help.

The therapist helped me unpack the emotions that I was feeling.

Document, document, and document: I started to write down my feelings and record microaggressive situations by typing them on a Google Doc. Writing down incidents and one's feelings can not only be cathartic, but it is also a great way to prepare for a future conversation or possible lawsuit. Documenting the incidents allowed me to process my thoughts and emotions. In addition, one should be aware of discrimination laws and university policies, as the microaggressor's behavior may not be legal or conflicts with the policies.

Don't limit yourself: A major part of self-care for me was finding an outlet and mentally clocking out when I was not clocked-in. Cheerleading was my outlet, because it prevented me from dwelling on the stress I was dealing with at work. I do not expect everyone to become cheerleaders overnight if they are dealing with microaggressions at work; however it is important to have a hobby outside of work, so stress from work do not consume one's life. Furthermore, as my wise professor once said, "you are always in the job market, even when you are not." One should always keep networking and have their options open, so they do not feel trapped. I told myself that if I was to leave my position tomorrow, I needed to have a backup plan and started applying to other graduate assistantships.

Or Should I Go: Making the Decision to Leave the Position

Listen to your body: As much as I loved what I did, by the end of the semester, I knew it was time for me to resign from the position. My health was a major indicator that I could no longer fight a losing battle, trying to change a group of White administrators. I developed serious health issues due to the racial battle fatigue and anxiety from working in a hostile environment. Sometimes one's body indicates whether one is uncomfortable with a situation before one is consciously aware, such as tensing of the shoulders or the feeling of nausea.

One day as I was booking a follow-up doctor appointment, I looked at my calendar, thinking that I can squeeze the appointment in between work and class. As I was trying to figure out the best day and time based on my workload, I tasted salt on my lips. I registered to fact that I was having an emotional breakdown. I got up from the table to grab a tissue and began laughing. I thought to myself: *"here I am, someone who is known for being strong, passionate, and resilient, who survived being homeless, the hood, and abuse, crying because of a 'job'?"* At that point, I became cognizant to the fact that self-care trumps my work because I cannot give my all if I am burnt out. I needed to step away from my position. I realized that I could still keep in touch and mentor the students that I was fond of, without compromising my well-being and happiness.

Bow out (not down) gracefully: Although I contemplated leaving my graduate assistantship for some time, I decided that I was not going to give the staff ammunition to disparagingly discuss my work performance. I ensured that I completed all my projects, not take on new ones that I knew I was not be able to complete by the end of the semester, and tied any loose knots. As much as I wanted to, I chose not to badmouth my former graduate assistantship to others. The higher education field is such an interconnected, small field, where it can be easy to vent to the wrong person. Furthermore, especially in interviews, speaking negatively about the job, looks poorly on the person more so than the job. However, I also felt that a major part of wrapping up loose ends was to let the students that I was close to know why I was leaving without going into great details. I wanted the students to know that I loved working with them and that I can continue to serve as a resource, independently from my graduate assistantship. Fast-forward a year later, I remain in contact with a core group of students from the graduate assistantship. Since I have left, they expressed their appreciation for my honesty and my strength to walk away from a negative situation.

Participate in an Exit-Interview/Reflection: If one feels comfortable and safe to participate in an exit-interview or reflection with their job, I strongly suggest doing so. Closure was necessary for me because I wanted my graduate assistantship to know why I was stepping away from my position. Fortunately, my graduate assistantship required a reflection meeting after every semester. My supervisor and I decided that we will write a letter to each other and read the letter out loud. I decided to frame my letter as an exit letter. I glad we discussed my experience because it reaffirmed my decision to leave. My supervisor reiterated how much I contributed, but was not part of the team. All her solutions to this 'problem' were only going to further marginalize me.

"Do as I say and don't do as I do,": Ways to avoid my situation

1. "Don't go for what sounds sexy on paper": In hindsight, I could have done more to make sure I did my due diligence in seeking a graduate assistantship. Even though, I was well aware of the culture of the campus, I could have done research on the culture of the graduate assistantship by having an on-campus interview and shadowed for the day. I would have been able to observe the culture and see that the graduate assistantship was an all-White space. Albeit, sometimes it is unfeasible to have an on-campus interview because of commitment; I wish I asked to skype with a couple of current students and asked about their experience. It is amazing how much can be conveyed by one's body language when others ask about the culture.

2. Assess the situation early: Looking back at my graduate assistantship, there were many little red flags that I ignored, especially within the first week of starting. I could have saved myself a lot of mental and emotional anguish if I did not try to justify their actions. Sometimes, assessing the situation does not necessarily mean that it's time to exit. It may mean that one should seek an intervention if possible, such as reaching out to Human Resources or talking to the head of their program. I should have spoken to my program's director about the issues I was facing very early on, to see if they could have stepped in before it was too late.

3. Be mentally prepared: As much as our melanin is a blessing, it can also be a curse. Being mentally prepared means that one should reaffirm their values and self-worth prior to starting a new position. In a perfect world, one should not have to be mentally prepared to feel marginalized in a workplace. However, it is sad to say that one can try their best to avoid an uncomfortable work environment where they may feel marginalized, but still end up there.

My three core-values (my religious faith, my passion for social justice, and cura personalis) were my driving force to make this decision to move on from the graduate assistantship. This experience had taught me to hold tight to my values and to not remain silent, even in the face of being ignored. Before starting a new position, I now make it a habit to reread my value statement and remind myself why they hired me in the first place. It makes it harder for a toxic environment to break one down when one knows that they are more than enough and the position needs them. Ironically, my graduate assistantship pointed me to Sylvester Gaskin's amazing philosophy that I now follow for any type of relationship that I form: I will continue to search for the environment that truly cares about me, not settle for the ones that just say that they do.

Showing Up: Owning the Everyday Struggle of Authenticity at PWIs
Authors: Jazzmine Brooks, Lyndsey Williams Mayweather

The experiences of Black women in higher education, specifically at predominantly White institutions (PWIs), are multi-dimensional, varied, yet interconnected. Black women are often viewed as hot commodities and exploited for their talents (Duncan, 2014; Thomas & Hollenshead, 2001). The chapter ahead will share the reflections and experiences of two young Black professional women. We will share our insights and hope to shed light on the chilly climate in higher education that many Black women face on a daily basis. May our experiences prepare, educate, and inspire future educators who may face similar situation while simultaneously encourage allies, majorities, and others with privilege to support and stand up for the Black women professionals in their circles.

The first year as a full time student affairs professional can be difficult for anyone; especially for Black women who may be navigating competing and/or conflicting values, culture shock, and racial battle fatigue. Jazzmine remembers the first time she received an evaluation stating staff viewed her as unapproachable and angry. However the data reflected the complete opposite, showcasing that she was highly available, committed, and efficient in work. In an hour long evaluation meeting Jazzmine asked her supervisor for concrete examples, and although none could be provided, the negative evaluation remained. Jazzmine said, "I remember my supervisor, who I knew hated her job and felt stuck, telling me to 'fix it or else'. I remember asking myself *did she just threaten me?* I arrived mid-year at the tail end of the resident assistant hiring process. I had no onboarding process, and little support from my supervisor and team members. I had allowed her to fail me countless times without a word. Yet, I was grateful and excited to work at such a prestigious institution. I thought I had been given a chance and took these issues I faced as the nature of our work."

Lyndsey's experience as a Black woman student affairs professional in Orientation, Transition, and Retention programming can be summarized in one word; Isolating. As the only Black woman in the office and department during her first year at a PWI in the Midwest, Lyndsey often felt spoken and unspoken high expectations and double standards placed on her. When she first arrived to the Midwest, from a very diverse metropolitan city on the east coast, she was also met with culture shock and homesickness. When Lyndsey started working in the department she started within two weeks of her White female co-worker who had also relocated to work for the department. The director of the office went out of their way to help Lyndsey's co-worker get connected to the community.

They introduced them to campus partners and really took this co-worker under their wing. Meanwhile Lyndsey was left to figure it out on her own. "When I first moved to the Midwest I was really excited for the opportunity. However, I was quickly met with the reality of 'Midwest nice.' Let me tell you, it is not actually nice at all; it is quite the contrary. I thought that being at such a prestigious institution I would be welcomed and appreciated for my talents. Instead I was constantly reminded, through microaggressions and blatant actions, that while I did add to the team, I also filled their need to have a 'diverse' staff member."

Transition to our current institution has been difficult. Although Lyndsey has two years more at the institution than Jazzmine, they each deal daily with varying amounts of sexism and racism. To cope in this hostile environment, various coping mechanisms have been employed by each woman to deal with the emotional fatigue and fear that comes with being a Black woman in this profession at a PWI. This fatigue and fear comes from situations such as supporting protest/cultural movements, showcasing our culture in our hair and dress, and simply being strong Black educated women. They each wanted to support the #BlackLivesMatter movement because it's salient to the core of who we are but also wanting to be mindful and not alienate students and other campus partners. Lyndsey decided to add the hashtag

#BlackLivesMatter to her signature and within a week was told by her department that personal quotes would no longer be appropriate for the brand. Showing up to a rally is not you just supporting your students but also risking campus partners perception of you as a colleague.

"I find myself being mindful of participating too much because I want to be approachable to ALL, but not deemed as a sell out to my own. I also struggled to be seen as 'one of them' because I was new and people did not really know me. There is that other expectation - proving yourself. Being the only one or outnumbered by the majority is a constant struggle of needing to prove yourself," according to Lyndsey. Not only are we dealing with proving ourselves to colleagues, but we are also having to prove ourselves to students, especially those who might look like us.

Preceding the most recent presidential election Jazzmine suggested to her division that spaces for dialogue and support be created for students but no movement was made. Shortly after, Jazzmine found herself working with a student who needed to 'test' her first. The student first felt the need to assess Jazzmine's Black ness by stating, "I'm from Chicago, THE 'Chicago';" searching to see if Jazzmine knew what she meant before confiding to Jazzmine about what the potential results of this election could mean. Jazzmine went on to share this student's experience, without attaching a name, to prove a point about the need to create safe spaces for students during the election. Jazzmine was quickly reminded that 'we' don't play that role and that the Directors of the Women's Center and Multicultural Student Affairs would be best fit to provide that support. As women of color we find ourselves in these conflicting situations where it feels as though we are being forced to pick a side - to put up or shut up. With hesitation Jazzmine could not hold her tongue because they were 'our' students. Although our university boasts about being a welcoming and diverse environment, students are seen and treated very separately. Even when there was no mention about the race of the student, it was assumed that student was a person of color based on the support that was being requested. This way of thinking was corrected quickly by letting these campus partners know that students of color are not the only ones feeling empty. As student affairs professionals we are responsible for the well-being of ALL students.

What makes the work of Black women in student affairs even more challenging is having responsibility and feeling the need to show up in spaces even more because of our current climate. In addition, there is pressure to conform and/or compete with others - women of color and other professionals - as a way to stand up and stand out. Wanting to avoid the stereotypes of being the 'angry Black woman', we have to be cognizant of our frustration and managing our anger. In today's office environment it is have become the norm to hear and experience divisive words and statements targeted at Black women. With this we as Black women have to be prepared to deal with such occurrences on a regular bases. For example, Lyndsey is often asked questions about her natural hair and must deflect requests of co-workers to touch her hair. How can one work comfortably in an environment where you are objectified? These words and experiences can directly impact you, your student, and your peers. It's exhausting and frankly it is hard to imagine Black women in student affairs moving beyond just surviving to thriving without good self-care methods.

Many of us have grown emotionally disheartened and fearful of again receiving the same treatment from White and majority counterparts. Isolation, whether self-selected or out of circumstances, continues to be enemy number one. We find ourselves smiling more at Black people as a way of acknowledgement. Just like our students, we seek a sense of belonging to validate our existence in these predominantly White spaces. These feelings highlight the importance of Black women, and women of color from all backgrounds, coming together to support, uplift, and empower one another. The Women's Circle helps to fill this need and create a community within our small midwestern town. The women involved with the Women's Circle bring a variety of life experiences and different backgrounds within higher education. These women have been at the institution and in the midwest for varying lengths of time. The more seasoned women serve as sounding boards and confidants to let us know that we too can get through any rough patch. Our Women's Circle includes brilliant staff, faculty and graduate students who identify as *women*. We are diverse in experiences, roles, and among many identities but we have one thing in common - where we work. Regularly we find time to get together, support one another, and feel part of a community. We are empowered.

This piece is titled 'Showing Up' because this is what do. As Black women we need to do for ourselves and each other. It is clear that there are multiple hurdles and hills to climb. Jazzmine recently spoke to a woman considered seasoned in the field of higher education, and it was clear that the continued struggle of a Black woman does not end at high ranking. The woman proclaimed, "Ain't nothing changed but the weather." What we can encourage is self-care and community-care. That includes taking time when you need it, always forgiving yourself, choosing your battles, utilizing support systems and not being afraid to correct others in a professional manner. Black women are told to practice being more approachable, less aggressive, more agreeable, and to develop a go with the flow mentality. We're here to say - be bold, be confident, and be you. Most of all don't be sorry for someone else's inability to see your greatness. Before you enter a room there are a thousand things to consider, and when you are the "only one" these thoughts can be even more overwhelming. In the end, remember your strength lies in your faith and in your ability - we need you and your students need you to continue showing up. You do NOT take up too much space.

CHAPTER 2
Cultural Competence Challenges of African American
Student Affairs Professionals

How to Keep Students of Color on the "Inside": Cultural Competency for Student Affairs Professionals in the Aftermath of the 2016 Presidential Election
Author: Marcellus Braxton

I felt a level of disbelief on the night of November 8th, 2016. I went to bed highly suspecting that Donald Trump would be the 45th President of the United States. On November 9th, I woke up and confirmed the suspicion I had the night before. Donald Trump would be our new president, and I would have to face my students, mostly students of color, that morning.

I work in a fairly rural area of Tennessee, where my county chose Donald Trump by almost 20% of the vote. I also direct an African American Cultural Center at a University in this same county. My student demographic at the cultural center consists primarily of Black students and/or students of color who are often at odds with the ideology of Donald Trump, his supporters, and his policies. On November 9th, without a word spoken, I saw the heartbreak in the eyes of many students. For them, this election represented something deeper than a change in politics. They had to face the reality that a Presidential candidate not only ran a campaign and attracted followers through racism, xenophobia, and sexism but that this candidate was able to win the highest and most notable office in the United States of America. Did he represent the America they would now have to face?

I spoke to colleagues, trying to explain why this election felt so different than others. Did they understand that the "leader of the free world" explicitly expressed hateful rhetoric against marginalized groups and won support as a result? Did they understand that the humanity and livelihood of students based on their race, gender, ethnicity, status, ability, religion, and other qualities was now in jeopardy? Did they understand the sense of betrayal students felt from others because of this election? Colleagues often replied that they understood, but, in order to keep students of colors engaged and feeling like they are "on the inside" with regards to the university and community in the months and years following the 2016 Presidential Election, I knew that the cultural competence of student affairs professionals must go beyond simply understanding.

Cultural competence is essential for student affairs professionals, but what does it really mean to be culturally competent? Is it simply knowledge and understanding? While those are crucial components of cultural competency, it has a much broader scope. Cultural competence requires explicit, spoken attitudes and behaviors that convey solidarity to those who have been impacted. In light of the 2016 Presidential election and its aftermath, where students of color increasingly feel fearful, uneasy, and ostracized, the time for student affairs professionals to become more culturally competent is now.

So, how does one become culturally competent? To become culturally competent, student affairs professionals can follow a five step process. First, they must **acknowledge** that an issue exists. Second, they must **educate** themselves on the issue that they are facing. Third, they must **universalize** the issue for everyone to be able to understand and empathize with the issue. Fourth, they must **create spaces for dialogue**. Finally, they must **publically speak out** as allies for the disenfranchised. The 2016 Presidential Election and the Donald Trump presidency has presented many student affairs professionals with an environment filled with a variety of different political views with a range of students of every race, ethnicity, gender, religion, socioeconomic background, and ability. In order to prepare for this difficult time, it is imperative that student affairs professionals increase their cultural competence.

This essay will illustrate how I propose to apply these guiding principles during the climate of Donald Trump presidency. Student affairs professionals find ourselves in a unique situation and those who lack cultural competence need to modify their behavior to ensure that acknowledgement, education, universalization, empathy, dialogue, and explicit speech all play a role in creating and protecting an inclusive environment for students of color.

Acknowledgement

Students want to be heard, and too often, students feel as though they do not have a voice within their own University. Students of color tend to represent a small portion of the student body, and oftentimes, there is a tension that comes with being the minority voice. When students do not feel that the University is listening to them, they feel compelled to react. And, their reaction can range from protests, petitions, a student bill of rights, marches, and other forms of dissension or affirmation in order to compel University personnel to listen to them. But, what if University personnel started listening proactively rather than reactively? If student affairs professionals are to make inroads with minority students of color and become more culturally competent, they have to acknowledge that an issue actually does exist prior to moments of tragedy or devastating events. As was widely reported, the 2016 Presidential Election caused a great deal of strife and conflict around the country. Being in a position where I work with students of color, a demographic that overwhelming supported Hillary Clinton over Donald Trump, I was forced to examine how to interact with my students in order to proactively encourage them to use their voice while acknowledging to them that there are issues that need to be addressed.

Acknowledgement can occur in a variety of ways: privately or publically, individually or in a group. I found it important to have private discussions with students, both individually and as a group, who were still processing their feelings. However, I knew that I needed to take my methods a step further and have a public acknowledgement of the issue at hand. In order to do this, I organized multiple forums, where everyone on campus was invited and could explore their post-election and post-inauguration feelings. I had to acknowledge that there were issues on campus and in the world that involved students of color that needed to be discussed. More than that, I knew that as the Director of the African American Cultural Center, I needed to acknowledge to the entire University that this presidential election created issues that impacted all students, especially Black students. When someone in power can acknowledge that an issue exists, it allows others to safely discuss and acknowledge that issue as well.

Because students of color in a university setting are usually the minority, they especially need the voices of student affairs professionals. Given that many of President Trump's proposed and enacted policies affect people of color, it is important to create solidarity amongst student affairs professionals and the students they serve. I am an African American, heterosexual, cisgender man, but it is important that I acknowledge the impact of policies that may affect other races, ethnicities, gender, sexualities, religions, etc. In addition, as student affairs professionals, we must also make sure that we extend acknowledgment to those outside of our own identities and target groups, especially as many other minority and/or oppressed groups face troubling times.

Education

Though it may seem obvious that education is essential to cultural competence, we must define exactly what it means to be educated about an issue. For instance, consider President Trump's first Executive Order entitled, "Protecting the Nation from Foreign Terrorist Entry into the United States", which banned the entry of most people from seven countries. The level of education that we, as student affairs professionals, requires must become more expansive than simply knowing the details of the executive order and what the effect will be. Being an educated student affairs professional means having an understanding of history, law, sociology, philosophy, psychology, and other topics beyond simple facts and effects. To become educated in the framework of cultural competence, student affairs professionals need to be willing to work towards understanding people, places, and things as they relate to the past, present, and future. For instance, understanding the role that xenophobia has played throughout history can help aid one's ability to respond to students who might be fearful or concerned while helping others to empathize with the individuals who are affected. In my classroom, I had a discussion with two students, one whose family and friends could have been affected by this order and one who previously served in the military, who held opposing views regarding the Executive Order. I drew a parallel to the xenophobia and nationalism that occurred during World War II with respect to Jewish refugees. We detailed how thousands of Jewish refugees were turned away because of the fear that they were Nazi spies, and we explained how what is occurring now could be viewed similarly. By drawing this parallel, the student who served in the military was able to begin to empathize because of the ability to look at history and see what the potential result could be and how that can impact people's friends and families.

Education means developing a comprehensive understanding of issues, which in turn, helps in a multitude of practical ways. Understanding how this executive order could have applied legally could help prepare students, their family, or their friends who need assistance. Understanding why people act a certain way based on certain emotions, feelings, or events can help inform a student affairs professional's competence in order to combat oppression and subjugation. This kind of education about topics can provide a structure for holding student forums. These forums provide students with an opportunity to share their voice, increase their understanding, and evaluate the nuances of the issue. Each forum can be based on a certain component of an issue. One forum could be about legal ramifications while another can be about historical parallels. Yet another could be about the psychology and sociology associated with an issue. Conversations often fail because they are not focused enough to capture the audience and provide them with an opportunity to explore the issue beyond a general surface level. Forums, interactive workshops, guest speakers, and service projects with or for the targeted groups are just a few opportunities to engage in meaningful dialogue and activities that help provide a deeper understanding of the issues.

This extensive approach to education will enhance the student experience for a variety of reasons. First, students will trust that you have an understanding of the topic. Second, knowledge that you have done research will make them more inclined to express their opinion and receive feedback from you. Finally, even if you do not see completely eye to eye on the issue, you have begun to cultivate a rapport that can potentially open lines of communications indefinitely with that student while providing evidence to other students that you have a willingness to learn and a willingness to engage in dialogue.

Universalize The Issue

Acknowledgement and education are two important components for cultural competency that are essential to keep students on the inside. However, those two components can only go so far if student affairs professionals cannot universalize the issue. Universalizing the issue requires us to convey the issue in a way that makes people transition from simply showing concern and feeling bad (sympathy) to being able to share in the emotions of others and understand that each issue relates to feelings that everyone can and does experience (empathy). Student affairs professionals have to work towards getting others to suspend their own judgments and understand that though cultures are different, many cultures have similar value systems. The student affairs professional can accomplish this goal by integrating exercises and techniques to create connections between people and the issues at hand. For instance, if we look at President's Trump original Executive Order banning individuals from seven countries, everyone may not be able to initially understand the severity of that action, or they may have some sympathy for those who are affected. However, if we can get students to focus on what it would be like to be held accountable or judged for the (real or perceived) actions of a few, they can perhaps begin to further understand the complexities and nuances of the issue. We can also draw parallels, give examples, and ask questions to get students to envision what it would feel like to be separated from their family, profiled by others, denied basic physical needs, or denied liberties, freedoms, and/or rights.

Spaces for Dialogue

Keeping students on the inside requires them to feel like they are engaged, like their voices are being heard, and like they are part of the campus community, which is why it is imperative to create spaces for dialogue. Creating a space for dialogue is not as simple as getting a space that is large enough to fit students. It starts with finding a space where people will feel comfortable to speak and be heard.

When discussing issues related to race, gender, sexuality, religion, politics, etc., creating a comfortable setting is difficult. Too often, dialogues become an "us versus them" situation, or those in the majority feel as though these dialogues are just an opportunity for the minority to attack them, while those in the minority feel as though those in the majority do not understand or care to listen. In many circumstances, the conversations tend to revolve around one group explaining a privilege from which another group consciously or subconsciously benefits. And in turn, the benefiting group becomes disengaged or feels attacked. In order to combat this, I often perform a "privilege exercise", which asks everyone in a room a series of questions, exposing that we all have privileges in life. I ask questions ranging from family background, education background, socioeconomic backgrounds, or even backgrounds from being a certain race, gender, sexuality, or religion that is not the topic of the current discussion. Without fail, every student can find at least one privilege that they possess, and they often have to reevaluate how they've taken for granted that they even had that privilege. This exercise also helps people understand that highlighting privilege is not to condemn but to express that we all benefit in some ways, and this dialogue is simply pointing out specific ways that privilege affects some and not all. These exercises help to create a more comfortable setting for dialogue because they help certain parties understand why some benefit from privileges and don't consciously realize it. They also help the privileged parties avoid feeling attacked because they can reflect on the fact that every person in the room has a privilege and openly acknowledged it in front of them.

Creating a space for dialogue also includes creating a mentality within that space where people with varying points of view will feel that they can address an issue without fear of retaliation. A space for dialogue is a space to debate and argue about issues, not to debate and argue with each other. In order to create this safe space, ground rules must be established from the beginning, and they must be adhered to throughout the discussion. Appointing non-interested parties to legislate will be beneficial because all involved would know that some level of impartiality is trying to be maintained. Providing a space for dialogue entails having a moderator who is able to steer the conversation in a way that is able to consistently address the issue, draw parallels, and stay on topic.

Publicly Speak Out

The final component for cultural competence is publicly speaking out as an ally. It is common for student affairs professionals to acknowledge that an issue exists. It is less common for student affairs professionals to speak out as allies for students, particularly students of color. Publicly speaking out as an ally is an important component of cultural competence. In order to keep students of the color on the inside, they have to feel that those in power understand them, can relate to them, can find some common ground with them, and will advocate for them. When I began to use my power by speaking out during forums, interviews, workshops, presentations, and in classrooms regarding the 2016 Presidential Election, I noticed an increase in students willing to engage in dialogue with me about important issues, even issues that were not related to politics. The importance of speaking out meant that the lines of communications with my students opened in ways that went beyond politics. For instance, during a private conversation about an executive order that President Trump signed, a student was willing to divulge concerns related to finance, family, and schoolwork. These issues would have likely not been addressed had I not spoken out as an ally for students. As student affairs professionals, it is essential that we understand that often times we must go the extra mile to ensure that students are comfortable. Although students are adults, many are still finding their place and enduring struggles with life that they are afraid to address with someone who is not a clear-cut ally. Ultimately, by speaking out on behalf of students, I have broken down a barrier that exists between student affairs professionals and students, and become an ally who will listen, offer advice, and serve as their advocate.

The ability to advocate is an extremely important characteristic to have as a culturally competent student affairs professional. Through the other components, the student affairs professional becomes immersed in the issue. In this final step, the student affairs professional takes that passion and ensures that the message is heard. Publicly speaking out can be done through conferences, word of mouth, essays, op-eds, speaking to administrators, politicians, or the community, and in a variety of other ways. The important part of speaking out is crafting passion and support to reflect how and why you're an ally as well as why others should be an ally. Ultimately, if student affairs professionals are able to effectively speak out and advocate for those who are disenfranchised, they will exhibit a component of cultural competence that is essential for ensuring that students of color feel heard and included.

Conclusion

Student affairs professionals face a daunting task. The policies and rhetoric that have emerged in the aftermath of the 2016 Presidential Election and during Donald Trump's presidency have created an environment on and off college campuses that have ostracized and alienated students of color. We must develop the cultural competence to keep students of color included and on the inside with respect to their college campuses. In order to become more culturally competent, student affairs professionals need to acknowledge that issues exist, educate themselves about those issues, universalize the issues so that others can relate and empathize, create spaces for dialogue, and finally speak out as allies on these issues. It is imperative that student affairs professionals take the lead and become more culturally competent in order to create a better environment where students of color can thrive.

The Struggle is Real:
Becoming a More Informed, Inclusive, and Intersectional Advisor of Black Greek-Letter Organizations
Author: Tish Norman, M.Ed

Congratulations! You have been selected to advise a Black Greek-letter organization on your campus. Yay! No, but seriously, as an advisor, you understand that in order to do your job well, your responsibilities run far and wide. That is, working unconventional hours, weekends, travel, the occasional social gathering, and so much more. The truth is, you wear several hats. As an advisor, you facilitate, counsel, consult, provide information, clarify, moderate, teach, listen, inspire, motivate, settle conflicts, and the list goes on. It's nonstop. As with any student-centered position, this can eventually lead to advisor burn-out. However, you press on, because often, you find your work very rewarding! You are dedicated to the progress of young people, and I want to personally applaud you for your time, talent, and effort. We know it is not easy. I congratulate you for committing to your professional development by reading this chapter!

Throughout my career as a college speaker, one of the audiences that keeps me very busy is the Greek community. Through the years, I have worked closely with members, executive boards, and advisors and have addressed hundreds of Greek communities from coast to coast. Occasionally, during our trainings, students share that they don't "connect" with their advisor, and advisors sharing that many students just view them as the "policy police." If I am not speaking on a campus, I am delivering a keynote at a Greek Leadership conference, and I love it! However, when I hear students say that they don't even know the name of the Greek Life staff...that is quite problematic.

I joined my sorority as an undergraduate and have been a member for twenty-five years. I am a sorority woman. I know the culture. I experienced the ups and downs, ebbs and flows of undergrad campus life, first-hand. Today, I have the pleasure of pouring back into a culture that helped contribute to a very memorable collegiate experience and that I am still a part of today. Besides being on the professional side now, training and teaching communities how to promote excellence, recruit exceptional members, balance scholastic achievement, leadership and personal growth, service and philanthropy, healthy relationships and tons of fun, having received feedback from students and advisors, I understand that Greek-advising is not a one-size-fits-all job.

Whether you advise one, two, or four councils, Black Greek-letter organization (BGLO) advisors should be of the mindset and skillset to support, educate and empower members to make better choices and recognize the necessary changes within their organizations that leads to development, sustainability, and results. Often times, providing the not-so-popular, but necessary advice that students need to hear is best, and that approach is most effective when BGLO advisors demonstrate the awareness, understanding of, and an appreciation for the historical and cultural significance and intersectionality of the students they advise.

BGLOs are very unique and complex organizations that can provide equally unique experiences for its members and advisors. It is critical to mention that BGLO culture varies from year to year. Culture varies by campus demographic, location, trends, maturity levels and more. BGLOs at historically Black colleges and universities (HBCUs) are often the focal point of a campus' social culture. There is no struggle to "fit in" or thrive on campus. They are weaved in the fabric of the campus culture. They serve a specific purpose, have distinctions, and operate differently than their fellow chapters at predominantly white institutions (PWIs).

Historically, the handful of Black male students at the few liberal PWIs that even admitted Blacks during the dawn of the 20th century, dealt with very racist and restrictive policies, forbidding them to join co-curricular activities on campus. This, subsequently, lead to the establishment of Black fraternities. While Black students endeavored to create safe havens for them to bond, academically support one another, and to have more meaningful collegiate experiences, at HBCUs, similar actions were being taken by Black women who began organizing in response the racism and sexism they endured as well. Eventually, this led to the founding the first Black Greek sorority in 1908.

The recurring themes of exclusion, racism, and "otherness" felt by Black students at PWIs, in many ways, is still felt today. Feeling included in programs, curriculum, class offerings, seeing "themselves" and their interests in the broader campus landscape. Very unique from other Greek-letter organizations, BGLO tradition is rich is culture and the significance of their genesis remains deep-seated for its alumni and undergraduate members alike. BGLO advisors that demonstrate an awareness, a willingness to learn, understand and acknowledge the complex culture that is coupled with this concept of constant struggle, will better connect with and manage the affairs of their students. Your advising style is critical. Your effectiveness in this role then, is determined by your worldview, your knowledge base and the professional responsibility you take for feeding your perspective.

In this chapter, rather than provide a chronology of the history of BGLOs, I will discuss four focus areas that are critical in acquiring, enhancing, and developing intercultural competency as a BGLO advisor. We will begin with a brief historical overview of BGLOs with scholarly recommendations, how BGLO advisors can be most effective in their role, and the importance of building a healthy knowledge base of the historical relevance, cultural nuances, and trends of these groups. Lastly, pragmatic recommendations that student affairs professionals can apply to increase the validity of their guidance will be presented.

History

To understand the need for and the concept of Black fraternalism, one must first consider their distinct heritage. Black collegians were highly motivated by the rapid amelioration of socioeconomic, political, and cultural progress of Black American during the dawn of the 20th century. This, coupled with the exclusionary policies of white intercollegiate fraternities, BGLOs emerged as organizations that fostered a unique culture of student involvement, social support and personal leadership. BGLOs offered a sense of belonging, community, and acceptance to its members, recognizing the need of community awareness, racial and economic uplift, and education through service programs. On the collegiate and alumni levels, these remain primary focal points of these organizations today.

As BGLO research continues to expand, an avenue BGLO advisors can take is accessing works from prominent contributors that educate its readers on the origins of the Black fraternal movement. BGLO research is considerably young—arguably coming into its own over the last twenty years. Some historians and scholars might argue that given the newness of the field, vast collections of literature related to Black Greek life can be difficult to locate. Yet, over the past twenty plus years, more texts, archives, professional trainings, interpretive readings, historical images, empirical studies and edited volumes have become more available to researchers and inquiring minds. As more scholars continue to examine BGLOs, more primary sources will be accessible. Here are three of my favs!

Ross (2000) would make a laudable impact on the study of Black Greek life as he presented an illumination of the nine BGLOs in *"The Divine Nine."* Including an exploration into their respective cultures, Ross included personal recollections, experiences, and future projections from prominent members. Research on these organizations' evolution, unique ritualistic customs, traditions, complexity, difficulties and cultural history was also addressed by several scholars, with Kimbrough's *"Black Greek 101"* (2003) leading the way as a groundbreaking analysis. Familiarizing oneself with pioneering works that clearly distinguishes the history and culture of BGLOs reinforces one avenue advisors can actively seek opportunities to learn more about the Black fraternal movement and increase intercultural competency regarding BGLO members.

Third, a task that Brown, Parks, and Phillips embarked upon in *"African American Fraternities and Sororities: The Legacy and the Vision"* (2005), would follow the example set by Kimbrough. By situating itself in the rapidly expanding historical scholarship on BGLOs, Brown, Parks, and Phillips compiled and presented an in-depth exploration into BGLO culture by turning scholarly attention to the important social and political functions of BGLOs, and the cultural aspects of these organizations like stepping, branding, calls, the unique role of Black sororities, as well as addressing contemporary issues like sexual aggression, college adjustment, alcohol use, identity, and pledging.

Though challenged since the early years of their emergence by campus professionals, scholars, and other Black public figures, the significance of BGLOs to Black America could never be minimized. Hughey (2010) states,

"BGLOs took on a vital role within various Black communities. They were an integral part of what W.E.B. DuBois fashioned as the 'talented tenth' –the top 10 percent of Blacks that would serve as a cadre of educated, upper-class, motivated individuals who acquire the professional credentials, legitimated skills, and economic (as well as cultural) capital to assist the remaining 90 percent of the race to attain socioeconomic parity with the rest of society."

While the above-mentioned texts can be beneficial resources for advisors to learn more about BGLOs, let us turn our attention to clearly defining what advisors are and what their responsibility is to be effective in this role.

Table 1.0 National Pan-Hellenic Council

Organization	Date Founded	Campus	Nickname
Alpha Phi Alpha Fraternity	December 4, 1906	Cornell University	Alphas
Alpha Kappa Alpha Sorority	January 15, 1908	Howard University	AKAs
Kappa Alpha Psi Fraternity	January 5, 1911	Indiana University	Kappas
Omega Psi Phi Fraternity	November 17, 1911	Howard University	Ques
Delta Sigma Theta Sorority	January 13, 1913	Howard University	Deltas
Phi Beta Sigma Fraternity	January 9, 1914	Howard University	Sigmas
Zeta Phi Beta Sorority	January 16, 1920	Howard University	Zetas
Sigma Gamma Rho Sorority	November 12, 1922	Butler University	SGRhos
Iota Phi Theta Fraternity	September 16, 1963	Morgan State University	Iotas

What is an Advisor?

Advisors are driven by a having a strong sense of student centeredness. You are responsible for providing energetic and comprehensive direction, leadership, and management to the organizations in which you advise. You are motivators. You provide excitement and a renewed vision to the extra-curricular student experience, while creating collaborative, sustainable partnerships across campus. You are developing young adults.

By imparting trust, accountability, and guidance, you help prepare them for the next stage of their lives. Through ongoing and relevant engagement and support, you emphasize that campus involvement, retention, and overall success are important leadership pathways. Advisors are liaisons, bridge-builders and connectors. You synergistically link the academic and non-academic life of students while simultaneously supporting their opportunities for growth. Let us now explore how cultural competency can help you be more effective in your role.

The Effective BGLO Advisor

BGLO advisors are extremely important assets to their chapters' success. For you to provide comprehensive support and direction to your chapters in numerous areas of operation, it is vital that you commit to fostering the development of the **entire chapter**. You are the anchor. You are the example.

You are the shepherd. You set the standard and communicate expectations. Do all of your students know you? Do they really know you? Have you carved out targeted opportunities to personally connect with your students? Is it consistent? Only once? Informal gatherings help build trust between advisors, thereby providing stability to the organization, even as the dynamics change. Year after year, numbers fluctuate, students' development levels vary, and membership and officers change, etc.

National and campus policies are updated and a culturally competent advisor is better suited when they are familiar with the policies and regulations of the chapter, set forth by the international level, the university, and relevant state and federal laws. As a culturally competent BGLO advisor, you, also recognize that the needs of your members may be slightly different; unique. Even if you are affiliated with a member organization or another fraternal organization, the cultural needs, approaches, and functions of the chapters you serve are different.

Sometimes I speak at campuses boasting extremely large Greek communities, averaging 3000 plus Greeks. Other times, smaller campuses where 300 is the average. In spite of the size and demographic, my sole objective is to always be as an effective, impactful, memorable, and motivational speaker/trainer that I can be. I endeavor to challenge, inspire, and impart new information to every audience that I step in front of. How is that accomplished? How do I succeed in delivering an inclusive message, with inclusive language, where each and every audience member feels relevant and included? I research. I research, prepare and immediately connect with an approachable, friendly demeanor. Let me share my journey toward becoming a more interculturally competent professional.

Throughout my work as a fraternity/sorority life (FSL) leadership speaker, I developed a deep curiosity about the origins of this culture. My role demanded and still does today, that I possess a deeper understanding about the **comprehensive** fraternal experience, in general, and the Black fraternal experience, specifically. My thirst for knowledge and the desire to connect with my audiences on a more meaningful level, motivated me to even make this my research topic on the doctoral level. I was concerned with identifying pathways that would positively influence Black Greek undergraduates—shifting the culture.

I endeavored to engage them in broader understanding the breadth of culture, activism, and honor of the Black Fraternal movement that stretched beyond their chapter of initiation. For this to happen, I had to familiarize myself with the history and culture of **all** Greek organizations. I had to research the cultural foundations of the majority White organizations, the entire National Pan-Hellenic Council, and the sorority where I am a member. In the same way, to be more effective in your role, you must research.

To be clear, I am not suggesting that you dedicate your life's work to researching these phenomena as extensively as I have. I am, however, asserting that cultural awareness and intercultural competency, in any field…education, healthcare, or finance, etc. is made possible through a process where professionals decide to learn to appreciate different cultures' values, practices, belief systems, and customs. This process to become more culturally competent is just that—a process. It does not happen overnight. It does not come by osmosis.

According to Strayhorn and McCall (2011), this process involves several introspective and discerning activities. Four key recommendations that I found practical and applicable to this chapter are: (1) scrutinizing one's own culture and how it affects the growth of their personal perspective, (2) spending quality time with BGLOs in informal learning interactions, (3) soliciting support from fellow student affairs professionals who are "seasoned" BGLO members, and (4) reviewing literary resources on BGLOs.

Before continuing, it is necessary to mention that increasing one's intercultural competency is not just for non-Black BGLO advisors. This work stretches both ways. To reiterate, I am a Black female FSL consultant, who holds membership in a Black Greek Sorority (BGS). I needed to be well versed in my own cultural knowledge and awareness of all councils if I wanted to be effective in my work. Researching was a must. In the same way, when stakeholders in Greek affairs can identify with, have a sense of understanding of the historical climate from which these organizations were birthed, and the complexity of their glorious, sometimes destructive and fluctuating culture, the connection and relatability dynamic between advisors and students may render more effective outcomes.

Throughout the years of consulting these groups, and to McCall and Strayhorn's recommendation of spending valuable time with the organizations, when I visit campuses and speak at conferences, I purposefully engaging members in informal "interviews" to dialogue during down time like lunch or dinner. We cover topics like what led them to go Greek, their chapter's culture, who makes up their chapter membership, academic standing, examples of impactful social activities, organizational history, chapter challenges, and what they believe to be their organization's greatest assets. These are great conversation starters and can really open the floodgates to building rapport and better understanding your students. Culturally competent professionals like yourself, can offer more relevant and effective guidance for students of color by implementing this strategy—developing cultural curiosity and sensitivity to their intersectional backgrounds and experiences.

Building A Healthy Knowledge Base

Imagine the new heights the organizations you advise could go to with a simple changing of your paradigm, a broadening of your perspective, and an increased cultural awareness. A shift in your thinking, a willingness to learn, and an effective approach could make all the difference in the world. To review these forces at work and to identify starting points where you can begin to better understand the intersectionalities of your students, let us explore intersectionality, recommended literature and discuss a few diverse concepts from both internal and external student affairs perspectives.

Intersectionality

What does "intersectional" mean and what are its implications when leading and advising students of color on your campus? When FSL is designed for philanthropy and service, community building, lifelong growth and development, cultivating friendships that last well beyond four years of college, and a massive amount fun, within the last two decades, US college campuses have witnessed a surge in diverse student enrollment. Sadly, there has also been a resurgence of student activism, in response to a series of campus-based racial incidents and hostile racial climates on campuses from coast to coast...often, with majority Greek-letter organizations at the root of it. How do advisors address these incidents when they originate from and adversely affect their FSL community? How does one empathize and connect more deeply to incite change? Then university and organizations have policies that will be enforced. However, advisors that reflect genuine concern beyond policy may have a greater impact on members making better choices.

Legal scholar, theorist, and activist Dr. Kimberle' Crenshaw coined the term "intersectional" in her seminal essay, "Demarginalizing the Intersection of Race and Sex: A Black Feminist Critique of Antidiscrimination Doctrine, Feminist Theory, and Antiracist Politics," (1989). The term emerged two decades earlier when Black feminists like Patricia Hill-Collins and bell hooks began speaking out about the white, middle-class nature of the mainstream feminist movement that disturbingly omitted the experiences of Black women and other women of color. Intersectionality, then, accounts for peoples' overlapping identities and experiences to understand the complexity of prejudices that they face. Therefore, intersections of social issues, chapter culture, public performances, student experiences, membership demographic, student involvement and cultural beliefs of BGLOs should all be considered. Let us examine a few.

Benefits of BGLO's

Mitchell, Weathers, and Jones (2013) addressed the history, culture, and educational outcomes of BGLOs over the last twenty years, and these scholars have suggested that BGLOs provide opportunities for connectedness with like-minded individuals, that they are conduits for academic success, and that they foster collegians' leadership development. In In Search of Sisterhood, BGS member Paula Giddings (1988) also identifies certain advantages of being a part of these exclusive organizations. She offers that they are closed membership groups, as all members must be invited to join, must be in college, meeting a specified grade point average, and must maintain academic eligibility to participate. She adds that because of the closed membership, organizations are better equipped to attract members who leadership style focuses on coherence and solidarity (Giddings, 1988).

Connectedness

In researching Black Greek fraternities, BGFs, as a possible mechanism of success for Black male collegians, McClure (2006) found that there were several positive effects. Membership in a Black fraternity provided a stronger connection to the campus environment, facilitated a more comprehensive knowledge of Black history, and helped members develop close bonds with other Black males.

Additionally, the role of Black sisterhood in academia in the 1990s was analyzed revealing similar results. Harris (1998) examined the impact of participation in Black sororities of 102 Black undergraduate female respondents, 65% of which attended three PWIs, and 35% attended two HBCUs. Harris began the study with what she identified as several key goals of higher education—developing social responsibility, preparing students for leadership positions, and gaining a sense of community service (p.282).

Several of the respondents revealed that they were drawn to Delta Sigma Theta Sorority, for example, because they witnessed the group's philanthropic activity in action on campus, which aligned with many of their personal goals. The collegians felt the organization provided opportunities for Black female collegians to make a difference, within an intimate space, that are often not available for Black women (p. 299). Her study also revealed five areas the respondents said had the greatest impact (1) community service (2) a source of leadership (3) self-improvement and spiritual growth (4) relationship building and (5) general education.

Academic Success

Patton, Bridges, Flowers, & Lamont, (2011) investigated the degree to which Black collegians' affiliation with BGLOs contributed to their engagement in effective educational practices. The study analyzed data from the

National Survey of Student Engagement, (NSSE) and drew from written histories, personal experiences and various publications, where the main findings indicated that Greek affiliated members at HBCUs appeared to be more involved than their affiliated counterparts at PWIs (p. 119).

Additionally, Harper (2008) explored the relationship between BGLO membership and Black student engagement in PWI classrooms. The study offered an explanatory model that identified collective responsibility as a dominant theme, which had a positive effect on BGLO members in class. He stated that a Black fraternity member emphasized the importance of how his academic performance directly impacts his chapter's academic standing. Conclusively, Harper's analysis determined that BGLO members repeatedly mentioned throughout their interviews how a primary motivator to excel academically, was the fear of individual or chapter suspension due to low academic performance (p.106). This was a clear motivator for membership to strive toward meeting their respective academic eligibility requirements.

McClure (2006) highlighted the importance of student engagement and campus involvement and concluded that involvement in co-curricular activities leads to greater academic success, the development of leadership skills, and higher retention rates. If campus involvement affords collegians with success skills in college and in life, then BGLOs should not be overlooked as just social organizations.

McClure argues that involvement in BGLOs can be mechanisms of success for any affiliated Black collegian (2006, p.70). Taken all together, advisors have the autonomy to constructively persuade their groups to promote a healthy balance of culturally-centered, academically-driven, and social campus activities. Show your support through a hands-on approach, personally monitoring your students' academic progress, as well as encouraging academic collaborations with other Greek councils (Harper, 2000; Patton & Bonner, 2001).

Leadership

In lieu of certain down sides of sorority life like "mean-spiritedness, excess, and fear" that often accompanied the former NPCH pledge process (Giddings, 1988), prior research also indicated that affiliation in Greek-letter organizations positively affects those students who are affiliated in areas of leadership development (Astin, 1993). Kimbrough and Hutcheson (1998) revealed that community service is a distinguishable characteristic of BGLOs, and there are direct linkages between leadership development and service activity. BGLOs are traditionally rooted in service, as they were established to aid in racial uplift and provide leadership for the race (1998: p.100). These efforts drive these organizations today, and bare no variation from the national requirements for graduate and undergraduate chapters. By national standards, NPHC collegians must meet required community service targets as mandated by their national program.

Another aspect reflecting the value of affiliation in BGLOs that Kimbrough & Hutcheson's (1998) study revealed was that BGLO members showed more confidence in their abilities to perform leadership-related tasks than non-members. In fact, an earlier Kimbrough study revealed that approximately two-thirds of BGLO members believed that their leadership skills were enhanced because of their affiliation with a BGLO (Kimbrough, 1995). Kimbrough and Hutcheson assert that there is a correlation between these findings and the smaller chapter sizes of BGLOs, compared to that of white Greek-letter organizations is significant. The small nature of BGLOs affords their members with more leadership development opportunities, which subsequently develops more frequent and greater levels of leadership ability to be refined (Kimbrough & Hutcheson, 1998).

Recommendations

The culture and history of the nine BGLOs are very atypical in nature, more than some of its contemporary collegians may be able to articulate. As such, tips for BGLO advisors like consistently participating in trainings offered by professional organizations, reflecting a genuine interest in the history and culture of the organization, cultivating a trusting relationship with chapter officers, serving as a positive role model to chapter members, and reinforcing to members that you are there to assess their needs and support them, are all positive steps in the right direction.

Regularly attending meetings, supporting cultural exchanges and encouraging communication with other councils, and even introducing yourself to other professionals who are NPHC members on campus all contribute to fostering a deeper bond with your students. This way, you stay abreast to the latest policies and innovative advisory practices, and the hottest songs that your chapters are strolling to! Yaaaaaas! Sure, assisting FSL in ensuring compliance with state and federal laws, adherence to University policies, procedures and regulations is critical. Providing advisor training to assistants and interns, maintaining an active calendar and so much more is what you do! You should be proud of yourself! I am, and I don't even know you! What I am suggesting throughout this chapter is that I understand that your job is not an easy one. Your role takes skill, willingness, out-of-the-box-thinking, healthy people skills, leadership ability, long hours, weekends, and the patience of Job!

The aim of this piece was to recommend pathways that BGLO advisors can take in providing dynamic and comprehensive direction to BGLOs through increasing their own cultural competency. The subsections that guided this work addressed the origins of the Black Fraternal movement, how advisors can be most effective in their role, and how to build a healthy knowledge base. That section highlighted benefits of BGLOs, how the effectiveness of BGLOs has manifested over the last 25 years, and what the implications are for these organizations going forward. The final section provided recommendations for advisors so their work is made more meaningful with a consistent effort in the implementation of their intercultural competency skills.

We now have a better understanding of what Black Greek Life offers to its members and how valuable these experiences are to the lives of affiliates. Belonging to a BGLO fosters lasting friendships, creates a lifelong network to the lives of their alumni, and promotes friendship and unity (Parker, 1990). By examining topics like why the history of BGLOs is significant, why, despite enduring challenges, they are still relevant and needed today, and future implications, this text endeavored to lay a foundation for incoming or new BGLO advisors, prompt further discussion and meaningful conversation among seasoned advisors, its members and associated shareholders, relating to the overall effectiveness of culturally competent BGLO advisors.

Advisors, student affairs professionals, and members should not simply explore BGLOs for their social prowess and Black expressive tradition, but actively engage in training and discourse on this emergent body of scholarship, and its impact that has positively impacted over one million members through the years. Current collegians and even future members, and most certainly, BGLO advisors like yourself, will benefit greatly with a deeper and more comprehensive understanding of BGLO history, their longstanding significance and the role they will continue to play throughout the walls of higher education in America.

CHAPTER 3
Racial Battle Fatigue Challenges For African American
Student Affairs Professionals

FUBU: The Necessity of Organic Safe Spaces for Black Women Higher Education Administrators, Created For Us, By Us
Author: Allison Smith, Ph.D.

Get so much from us…then forget us.
Don't feel bad if you can't sing along…
Just be glad you got the whole wide world…This us.
- Solange x F.U.B.U [A Seat at the Table]

Given the current climate of social justice issues pertaining to Blacks/African-Americans arising across the nation and on college campuses, it is important to understand the precarious predicament Black women administrators find themselves in. Black women administrators are routinely and repeatedly faced with the decision of "how far can I go to support my students' concerns surrounding social justice issues without jeopardizing my job?" During racially tense times such as these, campus diversity units are often touted for the work they have been/are currently doing to increase inclusion, decrease discrimination, and mitigate the effects of White privilege to appease student, faculty, staff, alumni and community concern. Traditionally, a large portion of that work (professionally and emotionally) falls on the Black women who typically staff these types of offices (Dawkins, 2012; Glover, 2012; King & Gomez, 2008; Guillory, 2001).

Being that "diversity" is the "job" of these *particular* women, how do we help *the other Black women administrators*? Who are *"the other Black women administrators?"* They are the ones on campus in the non-racial, gender-, or ethnic-specific spaces who bear the same arduous task, without the job description, support, resources, or presumptive shield of protection of those in the "diversity office." This chapter will provide insight on understanding some of the needs of the Black women administrators who are outside of the "diversity office" on your campus and ways to support their retention and emotional wellness during what can be described as a "new Civil Rights Movement" or at minimum a critical juncture in our national discourse surrounding racism and discrimination. Due to hostile campus environments and a lack of formal or institutionalized programming/efforts to aid in their retention, Black women administrators routinely take it upon themselves to create spaces where they can be surrounded, supported, mentored, and uplifted by other Black women. These spaces created by Black women, independent of Black men and White women, are created strictly *For Us, By Us…* some stuff you can't touch. In short, sometimes the best way to support the Black women administrators on your campus is to simply leave them alone.

"… and there's no other way for you to get there?"

Those words from my mom and sister (for the second time) quickly snapped me back to reality from the music-induced fog I was happily enjoying. Their question, with the undertones of concern and fear, was pertaining to an upcoming conference at the University of Mississippi (known as Ole Miss) in Oxford, Mississippi that I would be making a five-hour drive to in May of 2015. In all honesty, as a Black woman administrator at a Predominantly White Institution (PWI), who was born, raised, educated, and employed in Louisiana, I had *already* had those same thoughts. The thoughts of what it means to drive through the "deep South" alone as a Black woman. Why was I not as afraid anymore? I had already voiced my uneasiness about my family's initial concerns and received some support from some other awesome Black women administrators in the BLKSAP Facebook Group.

The support I found in BLKSAP was the kind that led six or seven Black women to respond to my post, offering colleagues who worked there, lived near or could provide recommendations. Each time I received a notification of activity on the post, I was excited to see what it meant but there was one particular notification that took me by surprise. A Black woman that I have never met invited me to join her for her birthday celebration on the Friday evening I was in town. I was taken aback and moved to tears, awed by the ways in which we Black women open up ourselves to support each other. Although I was unable to make it due to the conference scheduling, I will never forget and be forever grateful for Kristina's invitation to her birthday dinner. What

Kristina, Erin, Lydia, Crystal, Patience and Jennifer did is what *we* have always done: make space for another Black woman. We have always created space for each other, whether it be a private group chat, brunch, happy hour dates, or lunch "meet-ups."

As Black women administrators at PWIs, we are often used to being one of a very few (if not the only) in a room, maneuvering through a matrix of microaggressions and stereotypes while fighting off what at times seems like an impending bout of Racial Battle Fatigue. Oftentimes the support of our sisters is the only thing that keeps us going. For example, it is the way we instinctively make space for the Black woman that walks into a full room, as her eyes scan the room for a seat and/or a place of safety, with eye contact followed by a sigh of relief on her end and a slight smile on ours. Sometimes encounters as small as that (or an invitation to a birthday dinner) are what may completely salvage a day, week, month, or even semester worth of self-doubt about our place in the Ivory Tower.

Given the intersections at which Black women administrators sit (including, but not limited to, race, gender, sexual orientation), they are often the targets of discrimination (Collins, 1986, 1998, 2000; hooks, 1984, Crenshaw, 1989; Rosette & Livingston, 2012) even if the reason for the discrimination is not immediately clear. For instance, as I stood and introduced myself to a group of White men I would be presenting to and watched the eyes of many of them as they realized that I was *indeed* the young lady with whom they had been corresponding with for weeks. Was this because I was Black? Alternatively, would they have treated a White woman this way too? These types of encounters commonly experienced by Black women administrators are known as microaggressions. Microaggressions, as described by Sue, Capodilupo, Torino, Bucceri, Holder, Nadal, & Esquilin (2007), are "negative racial slights or insults towards people of color" (p. 271). whether intentional or not. Sue et al (2007) divide microaggressions into three categories: *microassaults* (overt racism, such as calling one the "n-word"); *microinsults* (back-handed compliments that demean one's race or ethnicity), and *microinvalidations* (ignoring the impact of racial or ethnic composition, and as Mercer, Ziegler-Hill, Wallace, & Hayes (2011) add "color-blindness" and the belief in meritocracy).

Recalling the aforementioned trip to Ole Miss, I was one of two Black people in attendance for the entire conference (approximately 100-120 people). The only other Black person was a non-traditional, male student. Once I arrived to the check-in desk, instead of being greeted as a guest of the hotel, the clerk asked was I lost. Again, I have to wonder if this was because of my race, gender, combination, or even something completely innocent. What I *do* know is that, I arrived "dressed to impress" with my crisp dress pants and university-monogrammed shirt, laptop bag draped on my shoulder, head held high and wide smile on my face; nothing about my appearance or demeanor seemed "lost." As if this initial encounter of the weekend were not enough, as I located the gathering for conference attendees full of White faces, several appeared shocked to see me headed their way. I, on the other hand, was not shocked because I had taken the time to look up each school's staff before the conference and was fully prepared to be the only Black person there all weekend. As I approached the check-in station and stated the name of my institution (a large, public, four-year, PWI with an extremely recognizable athletic program), I could feel eyes fixating on me as I bent down to sign in and grab my conference materials. *Yes, "the Black woman" is from LSU.*

As the weekend progressed, I met some great colleagues around the region who have turned out to be welcoming into our specific field. Sadly, it is encounters like the first two that weigh on the emotional psyche of Black women administrators in majority White spaces that chip away, incident-by-incident, at our desire to remain at certain institutions or in certain fields. Those frequent types of occurrences can lead to *Racial Battle Fatigue* (RBF), which Smith, Allen & Danley (2007, p. 555) define as "the result of constant physiological, psychological, cultural, and emotional coping with racial microaggressions in less-than-ideal and racially hostile or unsupportive environments." Although there is less research on the effects of RBF on Black women as opposed to Black men, RBF is literally a reason that Black women are becoming "sick and tired" (McCray, 2011; Smith, 2016). So the question becomes, how can Black women take steps to simultaneously mitigate the effects of RBF on PWI campuses, fulfill our job duties, service our students, and protect our #BlackGirlMagic (thanks to CaShawn Thompson, find her on Twitter – @thepbg), when institutions do not? We show up for ourselves, creating the space and support that has been denied for so long.

One of the "buzz words" in higher education for the last few years has been *diversity*, whether it's campuses creating diversity task forces, writing institutional diversity statements, or securing the services of diversity consultants. Although these tend to be great ideas, they do not always manifest in a way that positively affects Black women administrators at the intersection of race and gender, among others. Until institutions are willing to develop and implement diversity programming that goes beyond the surface to correct the daily microaggressions, stereotypes, and tokenism Black women face, hold community members accountable for violating communal diversity standards, and invest resources into the retention of Black women administrators, one of the best things they really can do is not to infringe upon the spaces they create. These spaces, independent of Black men and White women, provide room for Black women to support, encourage, and even chasten each other with pure motives that in turn can actually help to increase retention. It is those "stolen moments" to ourselves that allow us to be reenergized to go back into our departments, with our heads held high, tackling whatever comes our way.

During the chance encounters when Black women administrators are able to be in community with just each other, several recommendations can be cultivated to help in strengthening relationships, leveraging campus impact, and retention. Some of these concepts include *bridging* (Eriksson, Dahlgren, Janlert, Weinehall, Emmelin, 2010), *mentorship* (Verde, 2011; Jones & Dufor, 2012; Howard-Hamilton & Patitu, 2012; Blackwood & Brown-Welty, 2005), *community orientation* (Jackson, 2001), and *racially-influenced decision-making* (Smith, 2016). The four aforementioned concepts are in no way an exhaustive list but are a start for Black women administrators on PWI campuses who are looking to form and/or sustain community with each other.

Eriksson et al (2010) define *bridging* as a type of social capital where "involvement in a network with weaker ties that link people from different networks together and thereby become important sources of information and resources" (p.2) that is common among women. This *horizontal* form of social capital is commonly possessed by Black women, who often have the ability to reach "across" campus to make something happen rather than having access to reach "up" on campus to make things happen. As you mentally scan the various departments on your campus, it is a good chance that several Black women come to mind who you know you can call to get information from or to get something moved along. Those types of informal structures allow Black women to maintain networks across campus that are oftentimes unnoticed by the broader institutional structure, yet it is an example of how we continue to look out for each other and reinforce our connectedness despite our individual campus locales. Some ways to leverage bridging include: making the extra effort to connect, even if you are slightly inconvenienced at times; if you do not have the answer, helping to find someone else who does; and simply responding, whether you can or cannot fulfill a request. These three small things can go a long way in building, strengthening and maintaining relationships between Black women administrators on PWI campuses.

Mentorship, a mutually beneficial relationship between two parties with one being more senior or experienced in a particular area imparting knowledge and wisdom to the other party. The party on the receiving end is provided a "sounding board" to express their concerns and have their experiences validated, which is essential to the success of Black women administrators (Jones & Dufor, 2012), while being able "to establish a sense of community in a space that can be seen as very intimidating or discriminatory" (Smith, 2016, p.39). As mentorship does require a vested time commitment of *both* the mentor and the mentee, it is important to keep the following in mind: be an active participant in the relationship; be willing to be vulnerable academically, professionally, and/or emotionally depending upon the nature of the relationship; and, be accountable to each other and the relationship as integrity matters.

As Black women combat the numerous pressures that try to force their exit from PWI campuses, such as having to work "twice as hard," microaggressions, sexism, tokenism, pay inequity, and exclusionism (Smith, 2016), it is important to identify ways how we can make each other feel welcome on campus..One way Jackson (2001) suggests we do this that can aid in retention is community orientation. Ideally, community orientation is everything Black women need to know about a campus and local community that will never make it into a "formal" orientation curriculum; the location of hair stores, Black-owned businesses, soul food restaurants or places of worship, which beauty store has the largest shade selection of L.A. Girl Pro Concealer, local events popular within the Black community, and the occasional "run down" of "who's who" on campus. As small or hilarious as some of the aforementioned things may seem, ask the Black women on your campuses just how important those things are. Being able to feel acclimated to the campus and the larger community oftentimes provides solace and support the institution itself does not.

Lastly, allowing Black women administrators agency over their time and energy in how they choose to serve the campus community routinely results in racially-influenced decision-making (Smith, 2016). Oftentimes Black people, women, in particular, are "stuck" on random committees as a faux, surface-level representation of diversity taking time away from initiatives or programs we're actually passionate about. Depending on the level of racial centrality (Sellers, Smith, Shelton, Rowley, & Chavous, 1998), or how one defines themselves through a racial lens, it is common for Black women administrators to spend their service to their campus by supporting racially-connected programs and initiatives as means of personal connection (Smith, 2016). Again, this reinforces a connection to the institution that may otherwise be missing, especially for Black women administrators who work within predominantly White departments, at a PWI.

Given the current nationwide political climate, intersectional discrimination on our campuses, and the emotional weight of the fight for social justice, it is more imperative now than ever that Black women administrators not only practice self-care but take care of each other as well. Never feel guilty for protecting the emotional well-being and peace of yourself and the other Black women administrators on your campus. Unapologetically guard those spaces created for us, by us … *some stuff they can't touch*.

Interrupting The Narrative: Racial Battle Fatigue
Authors: Tracy N. Stokes, M.Ed., Joshua Fredenburg, Ed.D.

Disrupting the narrative is the mission of those who suffer from "Racial Battle Fatigue" (RBF). Pressures of overcoming anxiety stemming from the lack of equitable treatment in employment and everyday life, has proven to cause some African Americans, and people of color, to develop psychological and physical symptoms that affect their everyday lives and prevent them from completing everyday tasks.

Background Information

Dr. William A. Smith coined the term "Racial Battle Fatigue" to bring to light instances of microaggressions marginalized groups experience at colleges and universities across the country. Before we continue, it is important to define micro-aggressions to give context for this discussion. Micro-aggressions can be defined as subtle/cumulative verbal and nonverbal acts which could include insults/stigmatizations that target race, gender, class, religion, ability, sexual orientation, and other underrepresented groups. Sometimes these acts are intentional, but Sue (2010) asserts that many times those who engage in these acts are unaware of the stereotypical labels they assign to others. According to Dr. Renee Navarro, Vice Chancellor University of California, San Francisco, these labels are often a result of unconscious bias, also known as implicit bias. Implicit bias causes individuals to use personal experiences, societal stereotypes, and cultural context that encourages assignment of quick judgements and assessments of people and situations. Everyone holds unconscious beliefs about social and identity groups, and these are tendencies that categorize people into social worlds.

Understanding the effect of microaggressions and unconscious bias assists with continuing the conversation of how RBF can be debilitating to those who experience it. Smith, Allen & Danley (2007) assert that there are damaging emotional costs for racism and this conversation needs to be addressed at institutions and organizations across the nation. When in unwelcoming environments, those who suffer from RBF can ultimately endure stress that can become mental illness similar to what soldiers experience from being in the field. Also, researchers have focused on generalized anxiety disorder (GAD) when discussing the effects of RBF and the Journal of Anxiety Disorders reports GAD is diagnosed when affected individuals experience at least six months worrying about a particular concern (Dugas, Gagnon, Ladouceur, & Freeston, 1998).

My Experiences

When I think about the experiences I've had as an educator, a student, and a parent, I can definitely articulate events that have affected the way I approach my daily activities with my family, and the students I serve. For six years of my fourteen-year professional career, I exclusively served underserved/underrepresented African American students. Most were first generation college students who may not have the support which majority students, who attended Predominately White institutions (PWI's) could generally count on. It was my job to ensure students had the tools necessary to succeed as they matriculated throughout their college careers. I accepted this undertaking with enthusiasm and seriousness because I knew though capable, some of these students would not be prepared for experiences that come with being a college student (of color).

I have worked with wonderful programs which offered great support for Black students who attended their institutions. I can say my team and I worked hard to ensure services offered were thoughtful, organized, and meaningful. Accessible resources, along with university systems that value diversity and inclusion, are the tools that have always proved to provide the support needed to ensure student achievement and timely graduation. These are foundations that show students that the institutions they attend care about their success and will put measures in place to assist with their retention and persistence. Unfortunately, there are times students experienced occasions when their peers or professors failed to provide the resources needed for success. Many times, students came to me with stories of White peers not wanting them to be in their study groups, and professors and instructors requesting they give the Black experience in class. Organizations comprised of mostly students (of color) were not receiving the same funding and support as majority organizations, and students of color were not being represented or chosen to participate in popular retreats and activities sponsored by the university.

As you can imagine, students were hurt and confused when their experiences affected their academic achievement, social growth, and ability to participate in co-curricular activities on campus. Students voiced they didn't feel as though their experiences were taken into consideration when planning for their progression towards academic goals. They wanted administration to know they mattered, their concerns mattered, and they wanted to be included in more than just "multicultural" events, activities, and services.

At times, it was difficult for me to explain to professors and administrators that called me in reference to my students (of color) who were having trouble in their classes or programs. This task proved difficult at times because the number of students of color outnumbered the faculty and staff in place to serve them. At times it was not possible to address all of the concerns brought to my office on a daily basis. I found it exhausting at times to give students what they needed and explain to others why it was important to stop and consider that students of color are not the same, and shouldn't be lumped in certain categories because of their skin color. Because of my own struggles navigating the effects of micro-aggressions and systematic racism, I felt myself slipping into the mindset that things would never change, and I would never be the change agent needed to empower my students to look past the difficult situations and have hope.

Unfortunately, I was not the only administrator that felt this way on campus. Colleagues of color across campuses lamented that students were not receiving the support needed to succeed. I agreed with them. Sometimes it proved difficult to be on one accord with colleagues (of color) because they were not interested in rocking the boat. They were on the fast track in their career, and indifferent when it came to being the voice for the issues African American students (and other students of color). Faculty and staff of color were also often fearful of not speaking up because they did not want to lose their jobs. It was a difficult situation and though I hated the thought and hated to admit it, I understood their reasoning.

Fighting these battles for my students and debating with colleagues and administration began to affect me and I developed severe anxiety. I doubted my abilities, and I began to believe I didn't have the right to voice my concerns. I felt as though I didn't deserve my "seat at the table", and felt as though my concerns were watered down and swept away. I internalized it and the students witnessed it. My mental health suffered, my physical health was deteriorating, and socially I was withdrawn and rarely left my home. Stress caused me to pull away from my loved ones and caused extreme physical fatigue. I was slowly losing my passion and quickly losing my patience in search for a solution to guide my students (and myself) through this systematic maze.

Essentially, something needed to change, and fast. I knew I needed to regroup so that I could remain a great resource for the students I was positioned to serve. I knew that I needed to take the time for self-care, but I didn't want to be seen as weak, as ineffective. I knew if this continued, my mental health, my physical health, and my family life would be affected. I needed someone to hear my cry and help me fight this intense battle.

Solution

To help me overcome some of these challenging situations, I connected with a good friend named Joshua Fredenburg. Joshua is not only an incredible speaker and author who has been impacting the lives of students and student affairs professionals for the past decade, he has provided me with a few strategies to help me deal with the challenges of racial battle fatigue. Although he does not work on a college campus, I found his advice to be helpful and relatable because he is a man of color, and works with students of color as a national speaker. My hope is that his suggestions helps others overcome the challenges of racial battle fatigue.

The first strategy that Dr. Fredenburg suggested I employ, to overcome the emotional effects of racial battle fatigue, is strengthening my emotional intelligence. Emotional intelligence is the ability to identify and regulate personal and emotional triggers. It is also the ability to identify and effectively respond to the emotions and emotional needs of others. To move forward with combating racial battle fatigue, Dr. Fredenburg encouraged me to identify emotional triggers that negatively affect me, and develop a set of regulation strategies to combat the issues. A regulation strategy is the process of taking charge of your own learning, monitoring your behavior, and making adjustments in your environment to ensure an alternative positive outcome. His reasoning: we can still fight for equality within our spaces of employment, but if we don't deal with emotional challenges we face in the fight for equality, our ability for victory in these situations will be greatly diminished because we lose sight of the bigger picture.

In addition to dealing with emotional triggers, emotional intelligence provided the social awareness to recognize and help more students of color affected by RBF, because it would enable me to learn how to AVOID those who create venomous spaces which affected me as a woman of color. This strategy was important to me because certain emotional battles need to be avoided in order to ensure I am not emotionally drained from negative conversations and toxic workplace environments.

The second strategy that Dr. Fredenburg provided me with was to create a Daily Motivational Routine (DMR). He defines a DMR as a set of disciplines such as *reading, positive affirmations, prayer, meditate, listening to positive music, watching positive videos, and working out* that motivate you daily and prepare you for the unexpected challenges. The reasoning behind this strategy is that if I was able to effectively fill my positivity tank each day before I dealt with the expected and unexpected challenges, it would assist me with creating strategies to protect my mental, emotional, and physical health. Certain experiences are sure to be difficult, but having a routine in place would give me the strength that I needed to overcome the effects of racial battle fatigue. Thankfully for me, when I was consistent with this strategy, it made a positive difference in my life.

The last strategy that Dr. Fredenburg suggested to assist with dealing with racial battle fatigue was develop a strong support team. Although this strategy was not new for me, it was a great reminder because support teams were the very things that assisted me and my students overcome the effects of racial battle fatigue. Without a strong support team, I am confident that the negative effects of racial battle fatigue would have been worse. Subsequently, I encourage other educators to create a strong support system with mentors, peer mentors, and friends who you can share stories with cry with, and be empowered to make an impact in the lives of students of color.

Closing

I matter. My students matter. My colleagues matter. We are a collection of different voices, experiences, and abilities on a mission to make a difference in our world. We fight battles that attempt to define our experiences and strive on a daily basis to disrupt the narrative that systematically attempts to break our spirit. We persist and achieve our goals even when we are broken and think we will not, and cannot make a difference. Dealing with unconscious bias, micro-aggressions in workplace/educational spaces, and racial battle fatigue are struggles that may never end. I have learned that building relationships with those who inspire me to set goals, creating spaces for mindful self-care, and reminding myself that I make a difference in the lives of students I serve are strategies I employ to ensure success, even when it seems impossible.

CHAPTER 4
Intersectionality Challenges for African American Student
Affairs Professionals

Developing Expertise Beyond Our Professional Roles: Discussing Race & Privilege Within Higher Education
Author: Prentiss A. Dantzler, Ph.D.

Higher education professionals engage in multiple roles at their colleges and universities that stretch beyond professional titles. In some cases, their responsibilities include numerous actions of invisible labor. This is most apparent for those who identify amongst a long list of marginalized groups in campus communities. For many of us, our entrance into higher education centered on the idea of college as a transformational experience. In some ways, our journey towards higher education inspired us to transition beyond the role of a student to the work of an administrator or faculty member. This work becomes even more arduous as social tensions rise in mainstream America. For instance, the constant debates over Black Lives Matter versus All Lives Matter within popular discourse forced higher education professionals to engage in deeper conversations about race and privilege. Such conversations force us all to step beyond the basic tenets of our professional roles and teach our colleagues about the nuances of identity and our positionality within White, masculine, heteronormative, elite spaces.

Higher education professionals are also thought of as gatekeepers of knowledge. This knowledge often relates more to each person's individual identity versus their academic or professional backgrounds. Informal conversations about race in the workplace force many administrators of color to serve as "experts" on all aspects of race. The same can be said for administrators who identify as members of the LGBTQIA+ community. While our individual experiences are crucial to changing the climate of higher education as we respond to changing demographics among our student populations, this can lead to superficial conversations rather than the transformative, critical dialogue we hope to have with our peers and students. These conversations are even harder to have when 'administrators of diversity' often serve as a minute voice in their workplaces. Therefore, the question becomes how can we have constructive conversations about race and privilege within higher education? Framed within the lens of social justice, diversity is the easiest part of the work; the real problem is that most of us are inadvertently or intentionally tackling surrounding issues of equity and inclusivity. This chapter will explore the gaps in discussing diversity as well as how we can reframe conversations and develop programmatic changes for the future of higher education.

Focusing on diversity can mask critical issues concerning equity and inclusion of salient student and professional populations. If we are to be proponents of social justice and community development, then it is necessary that our everyday interactions within higher education exemplify these broader ideals. This discussion stems from a previous speech at the Mid-Atlantic Association of College and University Housing Officers Annual Conference in the fall of 2016. The speech in many respects was a call to action. And while the reception of the address was well received, there were elements of the speech that must be furthered within this discussion in terms of outlining actionable items for higher education professionals. Nobel Prize Winner Harold Kroto said, "I think the most important thing that young people should be taught at school is how they can decide what they're being told is true" (Palca, 2015). Truth is not objective, especially when it comes to issues of race, class, gender, sexuality, ability, nationality, or religion. As individuals, we construct our own meaning for how we identify ourselves within the broader society. Simultaneously, people formulate opinions about who we are, what we like, and how we act based on our image. As much as diversity is an issue that we perceive at the institutional level, it is most evident in our interactions with each other. Black feminist scholar Audre Lorde said, "The true focus of revolutionary change is never merely the oppressive situations which we seek to escape, but that piece of the oppressor which is planted deep within each of us..." (Lorde, 1984). The work of diversity calls us to question our surroundings while the work of inclusion also calls us to question our own positions within society.

Inclusion builds on the environment of diversity. Diversity goals fail to recognize how changing racial, ethnic and socioeconomic demographics can challenge community trust and cohesion among and between student and staff populations. We must ask ourselves *how do we elevate marginalized identities on this campus? Even when we say "our campus", what does that mean? Do we have a certain ideal student in our mind and if so, is that image gendered, racialized or sexualized in any way?* The work of inclusion forces us to go beyond the idea that diversity builds a better college experience because even this statement invokes a perception that the presence of minority communities benefits the majority. Inclusion would pinpoint universities and colleges not only as places of diverse interactions but also places of exclusion. The beauty in the latter is that these institutions can change, often, more quickly than their surrounding social environments.

As a sociology professor at a small, private liberal arts college, I am constantly reminded that my students have completely different realities than me. While at first glance, I can assume that this difference is predominantly along the lines of race, an intersectional analysis further complicates the distance between my younger, White, predominantly wealthy, female students versus my own identity as a young, Black , male professor from a poor, Black neighborhood in West Philadelphia. This difference shapes our individual preferences and in turn creates different systems of privilege and power within our institutional roles. For higher education professionals, navigating these spaces may seem quite problematic at times. The issue lies at the nexus of several assumptions. Administrators and faculty of color are assumed to be pseudo experts on everything concerning race. Female members of college communities are often left to their own devices to battle masculinity and misogyny. Individuals who identify within the LGBTQIA+ spectrum are expected to serve as advocates for their own communities. Such assumptions fail to address the positionality of administrators and faculty as marginalized voices on college campuses. Literary scholar Walter Benn Michaels (2007) suggests the trouble with diversity is that we learned to love identity and ignore inequality. Within our quest to embrace cultural differences, Michaels suggests that we failed to recognize economic difference. Moreover, we tend to equate economic difference as cultural differences, which Michaels argues can overlook the sheer nature of social inequality as an effect of broader structural changes versus the actions of individuals. To some extent, Michaels also offers a call for discourse to revisit our disposition with diversity. But action is what we need.

Having served in administrative roles within housing and residence life, student support services, and academic affairs, my "expertise" was always assumed. Such conversations force us all to come out of comfort zones. In many respects, it's a catch 22. While we may not always want to be social justice warriors, we internally want to have a voice at the table. Exhaustion comes from superficial objectives. Within every department or office, clear and coherent tasks must be outlined for higher education professionals to evaluate if their presence is needed. At times, the politics of higher education will undercut the work of social justice on campuses. However, some proactive measures can circumvent some of this obscurity. Our inclusion into program development and curricular changes need not be for the sake of diverse voices. Our presence within these areas must be for the purposes of elevating our ideas into practice. This is the true work of inclusion. Having allies within higher education only serves as temporary forms of assistance. However, having accomplices furthers discussions into pragmatic exercises. We must not assume that we all come to the table with similar ideas of what "diversity" means. For many, the ambiguity of diversity work is much more for the appeasement of the liberal masses versus the social change sought after by progressives. Following this identification of precarious actions taken by higher education, I will shift my focus to more actionable items for professionals to consider. These suggestions are charges to individuals, but can be attributed to department, offices, divisions, or institutions at large.

You have no right to be comfortable. This feeling of comfort stems from our perception of our professional roles as jobs and not careers. Jobs are temporary while careers are lifelong journeys through a specific work field. While a position may be temporary, your resume will reflect the story of your life. If someone was to look at your experiences, what tale would they construct from your background? Part of the reason our stories seem to be out of focus is because we are scared to create a narrative that stretches beyond a certain lens. The field of higher education may take us in very different ways. As a Philadelphia native, it was hard for me to accept a position in Colorado Springs, CO. The apprehension was not just due to the distance from family and friends; it was embarking into an unfamiliar region at a small, private liberal arts college. My previous experiences have only been at public institutions and as such, I was accustomed to a certain type of student. However, my role as a faculty member has morphed to be much more than a teacher or researcher. I have taken on other roles through which I find fulfillment. At times, this invisible labor will do more for your personal goals than your professional. When discussing issues of diversity, I've realized that many people dilute its significance to just that of race. Challenging your peers' perceptions of diversity will begin uncomfortable conversations to framing how your college campus can be an inclusive community.

You have no right to be intellectually safe. In a letter released to their incoming class of Fall 2016, the University of Chicago stated that it does not support 'trigger warnings' or 'safe spaces'. Its focus on encouraging discomfort gained it mainstream attention. One of my concerns with the letter stems from its conflation with the idea of safe spaces and trigger warnings. While trigger warnings are provided at the institution's discretion, safe spaces may include other forms of individual resistance from mainstream, dominant culture. At times, this type of self-care can be a form of self preservation. However, it does not excuse the fact that college is about exposing students to the unknown, to engage in issues and discussions that can be challenging. For this purpose, your intellectual safety, which a trigger warning would imply, is not guaranteed. Intellectual safety becomes a slippery slope when we conflate the ideas of intellectual freedom versus derogatory or "hate" speech.

My working definition of intellectual freedom rests on the presumption that every individual has the right to explore and obtain knowledge from all points of view. However, we must not confuse knowledge with truth. For both, truth and knowledge can be a system of socially constructed beliefs over time. While knowledge can encompass a collection of facts, skills and information through which individuals gain through educational and societal experiences, truth can be more of a complicated phenomenon to explain. The obscurity of intellectual freedom has offered spaces for proponents of social justice and opposition to censorship to debate about material that is insensitive to marginalized identities. In both groups, they are operating on this basis of their own notions of truth. Yet, I would argue our preoccupation with being politically correct can mask opportunities for intellectual stimulation and powerful discourse. It is by confronting each other that we begin a cleansing of our own biases to develop a more nuanced view of knowledge. Campus communities ought to be environments for the exchange of ideas for the pursuit of knowledge. Through a lens of social justice, we must also understand that certain knowledge has a longstanding history of being privileged over other understandings. Overlooking this critique can lead to a false equivalency of including hate speech and derogatory ideas within the space of intellectual safety. Such is not the case.

Our job as higher education professionals is to create civically engaged members of society. It calls us to be advocates as well as critics of the same communities we fight for on our college communities. It should make us question why we do what we do. As some of the biggest plagiarizers, higher education professionals tend to recycle campus programs from their colleagues at peer institutions. Each campus has its own culture, its own traditions and with changing staff and student bodies, we must question the relevance of these habits. My current department has a donor who provides us money yearly to bring in a speaker around social justice. Recently at a department meeting, a colleague and I started to raise questions about reallocating that money to other things such as providing funding for low-income students to travel abroad with their wealthier counterparts. Simple shifts in traditional practices can reshape efforts into productive ways. Remember, you were hired to bring new ideas to a position. You are charged with educating your peers on the nuances of higher education. While many of your colleagues will have great institutional knowledge, you have to challenge them on their presumptions of how best to construct inclusive environments for all students.

You are in a community that is telling you you're not brave and powerful. Navigating the politics of higher education is tough at times. And in junior level positions, many of us seem like we are powerless to our supervisors, to our deans, but this may be one of the most powerful positions at your institutions. It calls on you to be braver than anything. Junior level higher education professionals are usually more connected to the student populations whom they serve. With great advising, we can aid our students in becoming proactive agents of social change. This, of course, requires us to understand that the world of higher education is a continuous learning process. This happens as much with us as it does our students. Being a proponent of social justice means putting others before yourselves. It also means that at times, we need to remember that our students are adults. While for many, this may be their first time away from home, the expectations we hold for them should be at the same level that we hold for our colleagues. We are not to coddle our students from discomfort and ignorance. Instead, we should encourage them to embrace this discomfort while also understanding how ignorance is a choice. This is most evident among campuses where involvement of students is meager. However, this in turn creates a false sense of expectations among our students. Students should be the drivers of the campus community. It is our responsibility as higher education professionals to guide them through this process to self-actualize.

We must do an internal evaluation of our structures to identify opportunities and obstacles for change. One of the first actions any department can do is to craft or revise their mission statements. This should be done every four to six years to account for changes in student and staff populations. This is not a top-down approach mandated by managers and supervisors. This must be done collectively with all members of the department. Crafting a mission statement can identify diverse viewpoints at the individual, departmental or institutional levels. Instrumental within any mission statement is how the department or organization approaches this idea of difference. Again, this task forces us to ask the question: *why do we do what we do*? Answering that question will renew or define a sense of purpose.

If we are to embrace this idea of difference, we must develop conversations from an intersectional approach to combat a siloed view of privilege. While diversity is important, inclusion is where we need to focus as the identities of our students and colleagues change with each incoming class. This process will be uncomfortable. It will also challenge you to think of alternative ways to engage others. However, as higher education professionals, we must take brave steps to promote democratic ideals for the goal of social change.

Gay & Queer Black Men in Student Affairs
Author: Khristian Kemp-Delisser, Ed.D

Black men's collegiate achievement (or lack thereof) has been called "among the most pressing and complex issues in American higher education" (Harper, 2012). Harper (2012) suggested we might be paying too much attention to the social and institutional challenges that keep Black men from persisting and graduating from college. Consider, instead, what can be learned from those who have been successful; those whose "journeys to and through college have been overshadowed (p. 5)." I argue those whose experience have been relegated to the shadows are gay and queer Black men. When one takes an asset-based rather than deficit-minded approach, a great deal can be learned from the "interplay between dominant, usually stigmatizing representations of Black gay men and [their] resistance" (Mumford, 2016, p.1).

Some student affairs researchers and professionals have shared recommendations for policy and through publications and conference presentations on queer college students of color (Strayhorn & Tillman, 2013; Strayhorn, Johnson, Henderson, & Tillman-Kelly, 2015), with particular emphasis on their perceptions of campus climate (Kemp-Delisser, 2015) and cultural capital (Kemp-Delisser & Higgins, 2016). A few have disaggregated and centered the unique experiences of gay/bi Black men (Means & Jaeger, 2013). But most of that research is about students. The lack of research and stories of Black male higher ed professionals, is surprising, given that, arguably the best people to support marginalized students like Black males, are the professionals who share those students' lived experience and multiple identities (Poynter & Washington, 2005).

It's a little bit of both – Roy

This chapter shares the experiences of a small sample of self-identified non-heterosexual Black cisgender men. I am both researcher and member of the cohort. Although I interviewed each man about their careers in student affairs for preparation of this chapter, I am also a gay Black man who has worked in student affairs and researched the experience of queer people of color. I have often struggled to feel as if I need to choose to be Black or gay, with few spaces and opportunities where my identity is embraced wholly and fully. I seek in this brief chapter to carve out a space that centers the experience of people on similar journeys of authenticity and honesty. My professional and personal life intersect with each participant in ways that amplify, validate, and limit the conclusions. I will strive to share broad themes and commonalities from their diverse experiences and backgrounds, highlighted by specific individual examples and quotes. So it will be personal and professional, Black and queer; a little bit of both, as captured by the quote this section leads with. "A little of both," was a common response from Roy, one of the men with whom I spoke. After providing brief snapshots of him and the other participants, I will discuss how the experiences of these men give insight into gender, resilience, and professionalism in student affairs.

Meet the participants

The themes shared in this chapter, are grounded in interviews of seven Black men, ranging in age from 26 to 45. They all completed at least masters level education and several held doctorate degrees. They all attended or worked for a variety of institutions, from large state schools in the Midwest and New England, to mid-size and small liberal arts schools in California and the Northeast and Pacific Northwest. All names are pseudonyms.

Roy has worked in student affairs the longest, nearly two decades. He has always been an out professional, despite dealing with homophobia from supervisors early in his career. He manages to counter heteronormative spaces in small everyday ways such as putting photos of his male partner on the walls of his office and coming out to students in the classes he teaches.

Tim also believes he can't dismantle systems of oppression and bias if he isn't connecting them to everyday actions. He uses his privileged identities as a doctoral student to academically push for new research models that are grounded in the lived experiences of Black men and as a man to work against sexism and to honor and recognize the contributions of women in his institution.

James is motivated by a desire to make other Black people of all genders and sexual orientations successful and happy. He is a connector who cultivates a wide network of support and builds community on multiple campuses.

Ben walked away from his job as a senior-level administrator job when he realized his peers and colleagues had begun adopting the same values as the institution; productivity and professional reputation over human and spiritual development.

Ron is the newest professional. Originally of Nigerian descent, he infuses his life with dance and contact with creative students to transcend the loneliness and cold that can creep in during the long winters at his Northeastern Predominantly White Institution.

Marlon, the diversity consultant and influencer, is frustrated by the ways higher education limits rather than enables social justice. He strives everyday to speak truth to power and turn adversity and challenge into an uplifting story of resilience.

Andre's identity continues to evolve and deepen as he grapples with deep questions and strives to show solidarity and kinship with all students on similar journeys to reconcile their public and private identities.

Queer Black men are unique in that constellation of identities.

- James

A constellation is a fitting metaphor for a particular array of social identities that exist like stars in a night sky because they can be understood as independent separate points in space. They can also be grouped and labeled, depending on variations such as geographic location, visibility of light, and season. Culturally-relevant stories or narratives are often mapped onto constellations. The social identities and narratives of queer Black men are similarly dynamic and shifting.

Black sexuality exists within a matrix of racism, sexism, politics and religion. Consequently, labels often embraced by White non-heterosexuals are rejected by the Black community. (Battle, Cohen, Warren, Fergerson, & Audam, 2002). Although most of these men expressed comfort with the label "queer," not all of them necessarily used the word to refer to their own sexual orientation or gender. Nevertheless, I use the word queer throughout this chapter, as it captures the multiplicity and range of non-heteronormative identities claimed by this group of Black men student affairs professionals (Dilley, 2015).

The sexual orientation of the Black men whose voices

are captured here included queer, pansexual, and gay. All participants benefit from male privilege, although they described their gender expressions and identities in nuanced and expansive ways. Identifiers they chose included "queer," "Beyonce," and "murky." More than mere semantics, their gender expressions challenge traditional notions of masculinity and demonstrate that queer Black men frequently demonstrate liberation from the classic "man" box. Their gender playfulness manifests through their dress, language, and social relationships that expose the underlying gendered and racist assumptions inherent in our field's notions of professionalism. I, for example, personally identify as man but embrace "they/them" pronouns.

They are well practiced at negotiating and prioritizing their multiple identities. These men described needing to have a heightened awareness in order to scan and read their colleagues in meetings or professional gatherings. They ask themselves questions such as "What activities or experiences are valued outside of my work experience?" "How much can I talk about the recent election?" They enter racial identity spaces conscious of the signals they are sending with their language, their clothing, and their gender performance. What language will they use to refer to their partners? How formal or fashionably distinctive will their wardrobe be? Professionally they yearn for spaces in which they can be themselves unapologetically unguarded. Supervisors, higher-level administrators, and colleagues would do well to publicly affirm and encourage varying performances of gender, whether through dress or artistic expressions such as dance, writing and spirituality.

I'm too excellent to play games - Tim

Queer Black men in student affairs are Black excellence. Rather than hiding or concealing their identities, they demand their voices are heard and their achievements seen. They insist on living authentically and honestly in all realms of their lives. Several expressed concern about not recognizing themselves in the traditional deficit-model narratives expected from Black students or LGBTQ student populations. They were in fact, high-achieving, motivated individuals who felt the gay Black male perspective can offer a positive and unique contribution to the field. Imagine how effective academic and social interventions can be when crafted from the needs and supports provided to and by queer Black male role models, supervisors and mentors.

We have to protect our magic - Marlon

The participants' Blackness and queerness both help them imagine an identity that surpasses the sum of their parts. Both identities suggest the possibility of a holistic beloved community, lending a sense of purpose and shared identity with other queer Black men. The spirituality the participants exhibited was not necessarily guided by religious principles. They all had reached what Bryant, Isaac-Savage & Bowman (2014) called "evolved altruism," in which they "felt compelled to reach out and help others" (pg. 90). It manifested in many ways. For some, like Ben, it was about recognizing the humanity in everyone and holding a kind of "cultural solidarity," even with those whose actions he found offensive. Or an appreciation of the preciousness and wonder of life and through artistic expression like Ron and Marlon. They all felt like a common thread bound them to other Black queer men and a commitment to being moral leaders, which other researchers have found among gay Black male leaders in higher ed (Johnson III, 2017). We can all learn from the power of their imagination and faith in each other.

A seat at the table - Andre

Professionally the participants described themselves as lower mid-level, mid-level and senior-level. Their position did not protect them from the forces of homophobia or racism. In fact, the experiences of queer Black men are often shaped and limited by systematic oppression that is both institutional and internalized. Ron described experiencing daily microaggressions at his institution. He compared the daily slights to mystic Star Wars "Jedi mind tricks" that made him doubt himself. Marlon used the metaphor of "invisible hands of White supremacy" that seem to manipulate interactions and decisions at his institution. I personally frequently find myself feeling like the difference between my experience and that of my (straight and/or queer) White colleagues that I feel like we can't actually be working at the same institution!

This double consciousness can feed queer racial battle fatigue (Wozolek, Varndell, & Speer, 2015) but it can also spur creative resistance. For example, rather than considering his Black and gay identities as "two strikes" against him, Roy and Tim saw them as adding value to their professional perspectives on diverse student issues and needs. Andre and Ben saw their job as offering students and colleagues an alternative to normative masculine language, gender presentation, and even career choices. Their resistance could be seen in small acts from Tim supporting and promoting the work of women colleagues in the professional realm, to

James' personal decision to grow his hair long and natural. Andre described wanting to be a model to others but in a way that was subtle and unassuming; even subversive. He wondered, "how do I let them know without letting them know?" All the men wished their supervisors and mentors showed more personal interest and support for their lives outside of their job descriptions, including hobbies, talents, or family life. That kind of developmental guidance and support can open up avenues and provide more people of all genders a seat at the table of leadership.

Conclusion

Recent attention to intersectionality as an integral part of social justice and student affairs profession is no coincidence, given how our field has become more and more siloed. We would all do well to not compartmentalize and compromise our personal and professional selves. We must insist on our own excellence and demand a seat at tables of power. No matter our sexual orientation, how many of us feel limits on our career aspirations and future in student affairs because our gender identity or expression do not conform to rigid standards of professionalism? What do we have to lose by channeling our labor and personal energy into seeking alignment between personal values and the communities we are a part of? If the lives of just seven Black queer men in student affairs professionals offer such rich liberating contradictions; imagine what we can all teach our profession when we strive to be our most authentic selves. And imagine how are students, whether they be gay and male or some other combination of identities, can be empowered through our example.

CHAPTER 5
Institutionalized Racism Challenges for African American Student Affairs Professionals

Personal Storytelling:
A Tool to Counter Institutional Racism
Authors: Dr. Anthony Walker, Dr. Patience D. Bryant,
& Dr. Zachary E. Shirley

Institutional racism impacts student affairs practice and practitioners daily. Rather than shying away from these realities, we believe higher education has a responsibility to acknowledge and unpack the existence, influence, and impact of institutional racism on student affairs practice and the practitioners who have to navigate organizational structures. While we believe in the importance of institutional responsibility in fostering cultures of equity-mindedness, the focus of this chapter is on how three student affairs practitioners use personal voice to promote equity in educational practice.

Personal experiences are real. They are relevant. And they are a resource for institutions and practitioners to learn about and from. We aspire to use our personal experiences, reflections, and perspectives as a tool to empower others to identify strategies to support the navigation of institutional racism and organizational politics.

Biological races do not exist among modern humans today, and they never existed in the past (Sussman, 2014)

What is Race?

When one thinks of race, what do they think about? What images, assumptions, and expectations front-load the thoughts and perceptions of what, and who, race represents? These, and other questions may be difficult for many to discuss, especially outside of one's comfort zone, because the concept of race, although a primary marker of socially constructed identities, norms, and behaviors in the United States often remains a taboo topic to challenge.

Rather than ignoring the realities of these socially constructed notions of race and the realities of racism, we offer ourselves, our experiences, our narrative, and a part of who we are to you the reader in hopes of fostering much needed critical thinking, investigation, and discussion about race. For us, race is more than an attribute used to identify individuals and/or groups of people. For us, race is an intentionally crafted marker used to determine legitimacy, justify oppression, and divide society. For us, race is a socially constructed concept that has to be exposed for what it really is and does to people. For us, racism must be obliterated.

Race is, as Scott (1997) described, a pervading and perpetual topic and problem in United States society. Jones (2005), further muddied the concept and discussion as he noted that even after the examination of multiple definitions, "I still do not have a satisfactory understanding of what race is" (p. 612). However, as abstract as it may be, race is an instrumental piece of American philosophy and practice used to exploit and systematically oppress those whose socialized racial identity is not a part of the dominant culture (Sussman, 2014; Omi & Winant, 2009).

Racism

One might argue that race in and of itself is not the issue. The fact is that who we are as a human race includes many shapes, sizes, and shades of skin color. And if this was where the facts remained then race may not be anything more than an attribute of physical skin color rather than a pillar for power, privilege, and difference. However, while different shades of skin are a fact, racism is also a fact.

Bell, Castañeda, and Zuñiga (2010) defined racism as a set of institutional, cultural, and interpersonal patterns and practices that create advantages for people legally defined and socially constructed as "White", and the corollary disadvantages for people defined as "non-White" in the United States" (p. 60). In other words, racism (within the context of the United States) is the implementation of race for the purpose of affording institutional power and privilege to some (i.e. Whites) while systematically suppressing and oppressing others (i.e. non-Whites).

A key factor to the definition of racism is the idea of power. This is what separates the experiences of race-based discrimination and racism. For example, while all people may experience, or engage in, race-based discrimination in the U.S. only individuals who identify as White can engaged in acts of racism. Further, only individuals who identity with a racialized identity that is non-White can experience racism in the U.S. This is important to recognize because it highlights the difference between individual authority and individuals whose racialized identity includes institutional authority. Without such an explanation, the concepts of race and racism may be used interchangeably and also minimizes the concept of systems-led and systems-based oppression.

The power of racism extends beyond the acts of individuals to the institutional level through racially charged practice and policy. Stokley Carmichael and Charles Hamilton noted that institutional racism alleviates the juxtaposition of individual and collective racism (Wachtel, 1999). It does so by eliminating personal accountability for race-based privilege while also allowing individuals from the dominant race to reap the benefits of privilege itself (p. 32).

Narrative Inquiry

We all have a story to tell (Creswell, 2009). For some, these stories are not only told, they are also listened to and heard. However, for many, their stories although told, go unacknowledged or heard. For example, how many women told of their experiences of sexual assault prior to the #metoo movement? How many lives have been lost or drastically impacted due to the system believing the narrative of police rather than African American citizens? How many institutions ignore or discredit the stories of students in an attempt to avoid negative publicity and backlash?

This suppression of voice, specifically the narratives of individuals from minoritized backgrounds reinforces systemic privilege by limiting the telling of counter-narratives that challenge the dominant culture. In turn, narratives that reflect ideals and values of the said institutional culture are normalized and assumed to be both authentic and correct. As Alexander (2008) noted, one's personal narrative is always situated within the context of the master narrative, which is a reflection of an institution's culture. It is important to acknowledge the role and presence that dominant ideologies have in contextualizing narratives and the responses to stories told as well as to the storyteller. For example, in the U.S. race is situated within a context of White supremacy. Whiteness has been, and continues to be, the prevailing ideology that drives the values, definitions, and practice of race and racism. Even when working within a critical lens and trying to combat institutional racism, the content and context of what race and racism are remains situated within White supremacy. How an institution engages and works within these spaces tells a great deal about who they are, what they value, and how they are preparing students and employees to lead and engage with others.

Responses to stories and their narrators also give insights into an institution's culture. For example, in 2016 Donald Trump was elected to become the 45th President of the United States. The election brought a swell of joy, hope, resistance, and strife. Regardless of one's thoughts and feelings, it was clear that the election was polarizing in many ways. How institutions of higher education responded to the election – who, how, when, and why they engaged their community – in discussions about the election, people's thoughts and feelings reflect the dominant institutional culture.

The culture that drives an institution's leadership, values, and day-to-day modes of operation is often implicit, normalized, and seldom questioned (Bess & Dee, 2008). If a culture operates free of critique it is difficult to make any significant changes to the status quo. In turn, values such as institutional racism function covertly, impacting how practitioners experience and navigate the institution and its culture. While such cultures impact all practitioners, and create barriers to growth and learning, the impacts vary based on a person's social identity and status. As this ASHE (2002) report highlights, individuals whose racialized identity is non-White experience greater stigma and direct impact of institutional racism than their White colleagues:

> *Persons from oppressed cultures tend to live in a world that does not value them, marginalizes their efforts, erases their history, and silences their voices. Dominant cultures have an opportunity to see*

themselves reflected in textbooks, the media, and models in the classroom in the role of professors (pp. 92-93)

Although ample amounts of data and research demonstrate the presence and impact that institutional racism has on culture, climate, and practice, institutions are too often inept in their efforts to change. For example, although shifts in the racial makeup of the U.S. are occurring (Green & Trent, 2005), some institutions have not embraced these changes. Colleges and universities that have not committed to fostering a learning environment that reflects their changing student body have "done very little to transform their campuses, culture, and curriculum to reflect these changes" (p. 104). While institutions implement strategies to assess the readiness of students to be successful, it is just as important for institutions to be evaluated on their preparedness to teach an increasingly diverse student body (ASHE, 2005). If an institution is not able or willing to change the culture, what is an individual supposed to do? More specifically, how do individuals from racially minoritized identities:

1) Navigate an institutional culture that suppressed their experiences and voice?
2) Foster a climate that promotes critical thinking, equity, and empowerment for themselves, their peers, and students?
3) Integrate an ethic of self-care into their work?

So What?

So, what does this all mean for student affairs practitioners? How do we experience institutional racism in our work? How do we work to bring attention to, challenge, and ultimately change institutional practices to be less racist and more equitable? While we are not arrogant enough to think we have the answers to such questions, it is our hope to use our personal experiences as a platform to promote critical thinking, reflection, and dialogue among individuals and institutions.

What follows are a set of exemplars of personal experiences of three student affairs practitioners who acknowledge the power and impact of institutional racism on their identity and practice. A synthesis of our experiences follows the exemplars. We chose to write about our personal experiences, thoughts, and lessons learned because we believe in the potential of storytelling and sharing. As Clandinin and Connelly (2000) highlighted. "Experience happens narratively...Therefore, educational experience should be studied narratively" (p. 19). It is not our intent to provide a set of practices and procedures for readers to follow but rather we hope our narrative serve as a platform for practitioners to tell and examine their personal stories. Also, as noted in an ASHE (2013) report, a person must recognize their own culture before they can embrace and empathize with another person's culture. By integrating lived experiences into our work as practitioners we create opportunities to learn as individuals, grow as communities, and challenge structural norms that reinforce discrimination and cultural suppression.

Exemplar 1 - A.W.W.

"Nothing of me is original. I am the combined effort of everyone I've ever known." (Chuck Palahniuk)

First things first, I feel it is imperative that I enter into this space by contextualizing my social space, perspectives, and intent. I say this because throughout the tenure of my continued learning, maturation, and efforts to serve as an accomplice in the fight against injustice, I have become more and more aware of the impact that context has on content. Therefore, before delving into the specifics of the topic at hand, let me first provide a brief autobiographical sketch for you, the reader.

"When I discover who I am, I'll be free." (Ralph Ellison)

I am an individual whose identity offers multiple spaces of systemic privilege. For example, I identify with the following socialized identities (all of which include positionality of power and privilege).

- White
- Heterosexual

- CIS-gender
- Christian (more in faith and spirituality than religion)
- English speaking
- Not a person with a disability
- Non-poverty economic background
- And more…

What these identities, both individually and collectively, have afforded me throughout the majority of my lifespan is the luxury of not knowing. I didn't have to know, or even think about systemic privilege or institutionalized oppression because my primary social identities reinforced teachings and values of meritocracy, individualism, and the identities I hold. In turn, I went through school not questioning why I only had one Black teacher during my K-12 education. I didn't think about or question why church-goers all looked like me. I didn't have to look far to see individuals in positions of leadership and authority who looked like me. I didn't question things such as curriculum, pedagogies, and programming and whether principles of equity-mindedness and institutional responsibility were discussed, much less considered when making decisions. Instead, acts of injustice, ignorance, and silence were normalized. I say all of this because I think it's important to evaluate the systemic structures that influence how, why, and what we are taught. Does my upbringing and social identities linked to privilege make me a bad person? I don't think so. I didn't create systems of privilege, I was born into them. However, this reality does not give me a pass either.

Institutionalized oppression impacts all of us. Yes, the impacts are more direct in how they stigmatize, threaten, and impact individuals from systemically minoritized backgrounds. For those of us whose daily lives include a status of privilege, the impacts are very different. We seldom are threatened by institutional policies that discredit our work and/or qualifications much less our safety or well-being. Seldom are we in positions where we are expected to speak on behalf of all White people or give the "White perspective". Seldom do we have to critically evaluate how a new admissions policy is going to impact the demographic makeup of the student body. In short, seldom do we even have to think about being White or what that means. And this is where I would like to spend the next part of my time; discussing the role of White practitioners in being an accomplice to combat institutionalized racism.

It is certain, in any case, that ignorance, allied with power, is the most ferocious enemy justice can have (James Baldwin)

Full disclosure, I struggled a great deal with this project. A primary cause for my struggles is the fact that I, a White male in the United States, am complicit with systemic racism. My racial identity creates a systematized social space in which

I cannot actually experience institutional racism. Yes, I can be discriminated against based on the color of my skin (and I have examples of how I feel I have been discriminated against at times). However, from an institutional level, my Whiteness serves as a line of demarcation between experiencing acts of prejudice and discrimination versus experientially knowing and observing racism and oppression. And these realities created a sense of cognitive dissonance that luckily, thanks to esteemed colleagues such as the individuals I have the fortune of collaborating with on this project and a near and dear mentor, I worked through the process and found what I hope is a contributing voice and lens for this project.

How do we fight to bring light to, unpack, challenge, and navigate institutional racism? This question has been at the heart of innumerable discussions since my becoming aware of concepts and realities of White privilege, hegemonic ideologies, natural law language, and systemic oppression. And unfortunately, in many spaces the discussions have often reinforced the very attributes we claim to be working to dismantle. Rather than listening to the experiences of survivors and navigators of institutional racism, my experiences show me that too often the dialogue and decision-making is controlled by those whose social position grants power to decide (i.e. White people). As diversity, inclusion, and equity continue to gain traction, the system has often responded by rewriting and maintaining control of the narrative. Do I think this is performed intentionally? At times, yes. At times, no.

My experiences tell me that there are a great number of individuals in student affairs who have great intentions and think they are allies. However, many of these same individuals are often ignorant as their socialized racial identity affords the luxury of living behinds drapes of good intentions. Their (our) racialized identity does not require good intentions to transform into critically informed and aware actions. Rather than listening with an authentic ear to the lived realities, lessons learned, and perspectives of individuals from minoritized racial identities, too often well-informed White folk discredit our colleagues by questioning their actions; by interjecting a dominant discourse that they don't feel safe (which in my experiences often means we don't feel comfortable). We just sit back and unknowingly watch, and often engage in, Whiteness at work. Instead of listening and demonstrating an ability to be empathetic, we often fail to uphold the basic tenets of or institutional and departmental missions which focus on engaged learning, citizenship, equity and inclusion, civility, and more. Rather than teaching the values of an interconnected and engaged citizenship, we reinforce practice and ideologies that create barriers to learning and progress.

Exemplar 2 - Z.E.S.

Similar to my colleague, I would like to provide you, the reader, with a brief introduction to who I am and how my story fits into this chapter.

When I was initially asked to contribute to this project, I had to think about the perspective that I would come at it from. My story is that of an individual who lives with discrimination that comes at him from many sides.

I grew up in a great household, and for a good part of my life, it was a two-parent household, until my parents filed for divorce when my twin brother and I were in the 4th grade, only to reconcile and come back together when we were in high school. Academically and professionally, I have succeeded and exceeded many expectations. With a Doctorate on my wall and upwards of 13 years of experience Higher Education/Student Affairs to my credit, I am on my way to upper administration in my field. Speaking more on my profession, I have climbed the ladder from graduate assistant to a two-time inaugural Director of one of the most high-risk areas one can work in on a university campus (Fraternity & Sorority Life). Interestingly enough, I find a great deal of discrimination in my chosen functional area, for when I walk into a room of alumni from historically White fraternities and sororities, I am oftentimes met with looks of uncertainty, comments that question my credentials, and second-guesses to my input and expertise. I am on trial, whether it is admitted by individuals or not, every time I walk in the room, where I am oftentimes the one with the most professional experience, the credentials to my name, and the education and practical experience to further confirm my ability to do the work and know the world in which I work in. The looks, the subtle jabs at my ability, and the looks out of the corners of eyes by individuals who are itching to ask (along with those who took the liberty to have the "courage" to ask), "what makes HIM qualified to do this job?" all are a constant reminder to me of one fundamental think...

Before anything, I am a Black man

I wake up with this identity in the forefront of my mind. I am reminded through daily interactions, when reading the news and learning of the latest death of another Black man at the hands of law enforcement. I am reminded when I interact with non-people of color who question if I am capable of doing a job that I have performed, and excelled at, for more than ten years. I get looks of shock when people find out that "Dr. Zachary E. Shirley" is an African American man who oversees a department that, typically, one would expect a White male to be in charge of. As a Black man, I am automatically assumed to be a threat, even though I possess a 5'3", 157lb. frame. I can lay claim to many identities as one person, however, above anything else, I am a Black man. It does not stop there, though.

I am an openly gay, Black man. In the Black community, seemingly more than in any other community, being gay is a sickness. Something that is shameful. A "dirty" family secret that does not get discussed at Thanksgiving, Christmas, or the ever-important "cookout," yet whispers about my sexuality are laced within conversations about who made the macaroni and cheese. As a Black man, being gay is the last thing any parents would want for their son. In times where hypermasculinity and heteronormativity are considered prizes, I fall short.

I am discriminated against by non-people of color for my very existence as a Black man, and I am discriminated against by my own race as existing as a gay man. Conversely, while thinking in the realm of these two extremely salient identities of mine, I questioned where exactly "privilege" would exist for me, as I am not ignorant to the fact that I, too, have privileges that are not afforded to others. As I considered how to unpack the notion of my privilege, both for myself and for the readers, I came up with the following (which is by no means an exhaustive list):

- I am able-bodied
- I grew up upper-middle class
- I was provided with the opportunity to go to college for not one, but three degrees

- I speak English and am an American-born citizen

Exemplar 3- P.D.B.

My journey into student affairs is not the traditional one. I was not Resident Assistant who decided to go get their master's in student affairs, I wanted to be a professor and teach conflict and communication courses. I fell into student affairs while working as a student mediator while pursuing my doctorate degree, it was while in that role I realized that I wanted to work with students and I wanted them to see someone who looked like me on their side. I wanted to be an example of what possibilities there were for people who looked like them.

On paper my story is not all unique. I grew up in the suburbs of South Florida and was raised by college educated parents and grandparents who expected that all of their children to go to college. I went to some of the best schools and summer programs that the area had to offer and was able to earn my Ph.D. before the age of 30. One would say that I am living the American dream, but when you look further you will see that as a Black woman in America I carry a burden like no other. I proudly descend from slaves, domestic workers, sharecroppers, and landowners whose lives all make up who I am today. With that proud lineage I was always taught that I had to work two times harder than my White counterparts to achieve what they had and three times harder to supersede them. Despite being a woman, in my family I was and am expected to work hard and do my very best in all that I do, while remaining proud of my heritage and where I come from.

With that upbringing it is startling to see the very low level of expectations that others have for me as a Black woman. Being a Black woman often feels like being exposed and invisible at the same time. I have often felt overlooked and forgotten about when opportunities arise, or expertise is needed. Too often I have found that others have spoken for me in my absence or have disregarded my opinion on a matter altogether. Being questioned about my credentials, side comments and jokes about attire and hair or being asked to represent a whole population of people are not uncommon. When mistakes are made the spotlight feels brighter and the consequences harsher. The constant feeling of being a daily job interview where one feels as though they have to constantly prove why they have a certain position, despite listed experiences and possession of a terminal degree is not unique to just me.

Despite the discrimination I face on a regular basis I am not naive to think that I do not possess some privileges. These privileges have awarded me the opportunity to gain access to spaces that were not initially created for people of color and/or women. These privileges have allowed me to stand firm in my Blackness and my femininity:

- I am able-bodied
- I identify as a cisgender heterosexual woman
- I grew up upper-middle class in a very diverse environment
- I was provided with the opportunity to go to college for not one, but three degrees
- I am a third-generation college student whose parents have multiple graduate degrees
- I speak English and was born an American citizen

Synthesis and Lessons Learned

Our narratives and experiences provide the framework to examine the heart of our purpose for writing this chapter which is to provide insights into lessons learned when dealing with institutional racism and discrimination. The question is not will you, or we, experience racism in our student affairs practice but when, and how will we respond. What follows is our responses to a set of questions we developed to bring the discussion and focus full circle. It is our hope that our experiences and willingness to share our stories will empower you to reflect, share, and unpack your own experiences with both privilege and oppression.

As noted in the excerpts of personal experiences as well as ample amounts of research, institutional racism and privilege impact the daily experiences of us all. An acknowledgement of the presence and impacts of institutional racism on practitioners is included in the questions below. The responses reflect a combination of personal experiences and a continued process of lifelong learning and are efforts to provide lessons learned, strategies, and additional questions for student affairs practitioners who, as part of our professional responsibilities, have to navigate institutional racism daily.

1. What are some strategies that you have used to engage others in productive, solution-focused dialogue or practice focused on institutional racism and inequities?

It is important to consider the audience, their level of awareness, and investment in being a part of the solution to combat racism. For example, over the years we have learned that some people, for whatever reason, simply are not in a mental place that will allow them to engage in thoughtful and solution-oriented discussions about race and racism. Although it's a constant struggle, we have had to learn to be okay with that. Rather than spend time and energy engaging in emotion-laced rhetoric that counters facts and personal experiences with institutional racism, we try to use our time more wisely.

Progress requires growth and learning. Although our efforts have had minimal impact at times, the journey and struggle continue side-by-side. Each of our paths are unique, how we engage in efforts to promote equity-mindedness and inclusiveness in action reflects our personal experiences, narrative, and growth. However, among the midst of our separate and unique journeys are attributes of congruence. When we unpack the processes of learning through advocacy and allyship our experiences have taught us that approach often makes a huge difference in how discussions go. A few strategies that we have implemented that have yielded positive results and meaningful engagement include:

- *I statements* – "I" statements personalize discussions and situate us as an engaged participant in the discussion, experiences, and learning processes. We have found that "I" statements that include personal experiences, both positive and negative, often lower a sense of defensiveness from individuals who might enter the space with negative feelings and attitudes. On the other hand, "I" statements may also empower others to engage and share their narrative and lived experiences with others.
- *Institutional Approach* – Focusing on the systemic or institutional culture rather than the individual (when appropriate) contextualizes discussions around acts of the institution rather

than the individual. By situating dialogue as part of a larger structure, discussions can utilize a balanced approach between cultural attributes such as policy, governance, curriculum, and the various spaces individuals hold within those institutional structures.

- *Ask "what if"* – Asking the simple question, "what if the experiences described by individuals from non-White racialized identities are true?" serves as a neutralizing question. It emphasizes the experiences of individuals from oppressed and minoritized backgrounds without placing White people in a position to defend their actions. The question also creates an opportunity for voices that are often suppressed to be heard.

- *Objective Subjectivity* – Privilege allows individuals to ignore or create alternative facts when convenient. When engaging in dialogue focused on solutions, using factual evidence yields to an objective based discussion rather than emotions.

2. In terms of self-care, what are some strategies or personal practices (at work or outside) that you engage in to combat institutional racism?

Self-care is of the upmost importance for all of us. However, for individuals from minoritized identities, we believe the impacts of institutional racism carry more weight and directly impact individuals more. A few examples of activities that we engage in that have proven helpful include:

- Working out / yoga
- Social circles with individuals outside the context of the work
- Disengaging from social media, news, and the work after a set time in the evening
- Reading for pleasure
- Taking vacations

3. As an individual whose identity includes social positions that afford systemic privilege as well as systemic oppressions, how does your awareness of both socialized spaces contribute to your practice and impact?

For us, working to unpack systems of privilege effectively requires a lens of intersectionality. Intersectionality brings attention to the perplexing subtleties of difference and the commonalities of sameness situated within the context of equity and antidiscrimination (Cho, Crenshaw, & McCall,

2013). As individuals, we all hold social spaces that afford us privilege at times while at other times our identities include spaces of oppressions. An awareness of how these dynamics, juxtapositions of similarities and variances of our multiple socialized identities, fosters our personal narrative and sense of identity, increases our capacity to personalize learning and discussions, and empowers us to demonstrate empathy for others when our identity is one of privilege. By continuing to expand a personal awareness of systematized privilege and identity development, we place ourselves in positions to teach, lead, and learn in more impactful and engaging ways.

Concluding Thoughts

You don't fear people whose story you know (Margaret Wheatley)

Higher education has the potential to shape the future of our society (Chambers, 2005). However, the potential to lead toward a more democratic and equitable society is limited as long as racism is permitted to go unquestioned and unchallenged in institutional values, policy, and practice. What does this mean for student affairs practitioners who 1) experience and navigate institutional racism daily, and 2) want to impact change, foster a culture of inclusiveness, and cultivate principles of educational-equity in practice? Although the solutions are vast, personal, and in many ways situational based on context, resources, and experiences, we believe that an intentional focus on augmenting a personal sense of self, fostering self-care, and using our personal voice offer a place to start. It is our hope that by sharing snippets of our personal experiences we have provided examples of how personal voice and experiences can be utilized as tools for teaching, learning, and combatting institutionalized racism.

Merging Reality and Perception
Author: LaToya René Robertson

The world of student affairs is an interesting place. One filled with wonderful student interactions, teachable moments, and the fulfilling awe of watching students develop before your eyes. Like any career, at times, it's not all glitz and glamour. I don't say this to sound grim, rather to be transparent about the challenges that I have faced and have overcome. Before I get into this section, I want to first acknowledge that I had a wonderful time in my field both with my students and colleagues. 85-90% is wonderful. In this I will share the 10-15% that wasn't so wonderful and how I navigated those few moments.

How did my student affairs journey begin? I'm glad you asked. I began my journey in student affairs as a student. I served as an RA for 3 years before moving off campus. After graduating I was offered a position as Resident Coordinator and Director of First Year Experience. Later I moved to a different institution with a similar role. One of the things I noticed quickly was that unlike when I was a student, I wasn't encouraged to pursue all of my ideas and was often met with criticism of thinking too big. People assumed I was not capable of completing any portion of the project I envisioned. I was never directly told 'no' for any of my ideas that would benefit the school but the language used often had the undertone of "That's cute honey, you can try if you want to but you won't make it very far." The fascinating part of the undertone was it was common knowledge that I have a dual career and had accomplished a fair amount of things outside of the student affairs world both as a student leader and as a professional. I noticed that on occasion there was favoritism and a highly politicized structure in place. Me being the superior Uno and Spades player that I am, I quickly realized strategy must be used to win this game. Any goal I wanted to achieve could not be done in a traditional way. No shortcuts could be used for me. I observed that many key players in my goals had limiting mindsets and that the people above me would agree to be of service as long as their image wasn't challenged and the end result would make them look good.

My goal is to make the college experience an amazing one. Students don't always get to attend their first choice but part of my responsibility is to make them feel like this was their best choice. My mission was to make sure I was completing my responsibility to its fullest extent. My plan to accomplish my mission began with simply meeting people and seeing what their thoughts were through asking questions. How did they arrive at their position? What motivates them to stay? Are they filled with passion? Are they disenchanted? Do they have purpose in what they do? Is this just a check? What is their next step professionally and personally? Can this be a mentor to me? Do our views align? Is there natural chemistry? This portion of the plan is essential because you want to know what makes the people you work with tick. I also wanted to identify who will be members of my team and who will be adversaries be it intentional or the effort to call me just to say hello." It's important to understand that we work with people and the first step to getting anything done is to connect with them as a human being. At many institutions of higher learning staff members are not always acknowledged as human beings. That simple effort even if you don't directly work with someone can make a HUGE difference. If you take this approach, be genuine.

While I was executing my plan I would share with my superiors that I was meeting with various people across campus and picking their brain. After maybe my 5th meeting mentioned a concern was raised about me getting my core tasks completed. I was puzzled because I was often doing more than what was expected of me. I would volunteer to help when asked and the room fell silent. When peers used the reasons of having family obligations or class, I would accept the responsibility when I had the same level (though different) of obligations. I may not have been talking about what I was doing for my core position nor was I putting it on my calendar for the world to see, but I was not twiddling my thumbs watching cat videos in my office. My understanding was and is, get your job done. You can't always plot that on a calendar. One of the statements mentioned was "We don't want to be paying you to be a DJ. You are doing too much outside of your department". The off the cuff remark struck me as odd because I played music for an event for a committee that my department placed me on. At that point I had ONLY played music for events that my department assigned to me. I asked myself "What exactly am I doing that is outside of the department? Are all 24 hours of my day supposed to be dedicated to my job?" Everything extra that I was doing was on my own time. I often skipped lunch or worked extra hours to ensure that my tasks were done within human limits. (I am certainly one to test human limits!) I asked myself, based on what was said, what does my superior THINK I'm doing? They think I'm DJing, they think I'm taking on too much. The perception is I'm involved everywhere else but not at home. Once I came to those conclusions I decide to do conduct an experiment. The experiment was to keep doing the same thing but putting everything I do on my calendar, to stop sharing the extra things I'm doing on campus, share every single thing that could potentially slow down visible progress, over communicate, and take note of the results.

When I made the resolution to conduct the experiment I was assigned to two new large tasks. I know you're just as puzzled as I was. Why would I be assigned to new things when the perception is I'm doing too much and I was JUST reprimanded for being too involved?! I was confused and angry for several days. After those emotions decreased, I proceeded with my experiment. I filled my calendar. I included things like "walk to meeting", "check voicemails" and other mundane tasks. I stopped talking about the meetings or ideas I had with my direct supervisors and would meet with people I developed relationships with when I was in the "meeting people" phase of my plan. The people I would meet with were often people that I had natural chemistry with or served as my mentors and had a passion in them. Something else I always kept in mind was what can I bring to their table? I make it my personal policy to not just ask for resources but to also be a resource. I would share my ideas with the member of my team and they would often become excited because, it would serve their mission too. In the process I would also ensure that my department was attached to the project, big or small. As a result, students were served, my goals were accomplished and my once biggest skeptics became my best allies. Rather than me coming to them, sometimes they came to me with ideas or questions. When I would ask a question I was no longer met with fierce opposition, I was met with support.

I'm sure you're wondering what the findings of my experiment were. Several months after the experiment began I was told "I see that you are scaling back on outside tasks and focusing more on your core tasks." The reality was the only thing that changed was their perception and how I contributed to it.

Let's break down what happened over that time period.

There were microaggressions and biases that caused some authentic challenges for me. I had what was deemed as an entry level position, I was often the only woman of color, I was often times the youngest in the room. Outside of student affairs I have toured internationally, produced music on major television networks, and negotiated million dollar agreements. In student affairs I have created pilot programs, acquired hundreds of thousands of dollars for student life improvements, and facilitated around 1,200 programs. Despite my impressive resume that indicates "I get things done" I was treated like a toddler that eats playdoh and needs her hand held. My ideas, though logical and not all that much work, were shot down. I had to find way to get what I wanted done without being disrespectful, while making my department looking good and (for my own satisfaction) saying "I told you so." The oppression I received was either from a system of daunting paperwork and policy, superiors of color, or disenchanted people. How did I accomplish my goals? I took a step back and asked in the simplest terms What type of people am I dealing with? What do people want at the core? Who do I need to deal with, and how do I keep the most people happy while getting done what I need to get done? How do I remain true to myself? I learned when to share my opinion. My opinion does not always need to be shared. I tried to be mindful of my body language. I continue to fail at that task. Keyword here is "try". I am selective about the battles I fight.

Every battle does not need to be fought by me. That is a struggle because I am passionate. When I fight battles I don't go in for ferocious victory that leaves egos wounded, I go for technical wins that leave egos intact. Scorning people will not serve you well. Unless you plan to leave the position immediately after your victory you WILL have to work with anyone you were in battle with again. When things don't make sense, focus on the operational items to make the process more efficient. You want buy in. I learned my campus and secured allies. Understand that people are people and they have feelings. Make the students your goal but make sure you are bringing something to the table too. It's not personal, its business. Perception is everything. When you leave a place, leave your legacy.

As stated before, what was shared was a small fraction of my student affairs experience. You may encounter this, you may not. We also cannot ignore ways that I contributed to my challenges. My approach due to difference in cultural expectations from myself and the institution was a factor. My dream larger than life approach was a factor. Personality clashes may have been a factor as well. Hopefully I didn't scare you away from student affairs. That certainly wasn't my intent. Though I have had some negative experiences and, I have also met some phenomenal people and we created terrific memories. I have learned a lot about myself and have grown in the process. What I do, doesn't feel like work. I love the environment I work in and I enjoy the people I work with. I have no regrets about my field choice. Even with the experiences I shared, if I could go back in time, I would do it again. Good luck!

CHAPTER 6
Microaggressions, Macroaggressions, Stereotypes, and Biases Challenges for African American Student Affairs Professionals

For Brothers: Developmental Struggles of
Black Male Graduate Students
Authors: Donald Gilliam, B.S, Michael J. Seaberry, MA.,
Brandon Jamaal Stroud, MS, Michael R. Williams, M.S

Abstract: It is important that student affairs administrators are equipped with the knowledge and tools to address the unique needs of Black male graduate students within their institutions. More importantly, for administrators to challenge their personal lens and understand how various life paths and experiences can impact a student developmentally. The goal of this chapter is draw attention to the often overlooked student affairs professional, the graduate student, during times of crisis. The experiences of Black male graduate students exist in an unclear gray area between not being labeled "professional staff" and not being able to assume the full role of "student." This professional limbo can create apprehension amongst graduate students when they wish to express their own concerns and opinions while still serving as a resource and advocate for undergraduate students. With the state of current campus issues, the authors address crisis management strategies and self care techniques that Black male graduate students can adopt as they find the balance between their work, school, and personal lives.

Institutional Example

Educated Black men often face the challenge of daily microaggressions and stereotypes that create biases when entering into the professional field. For many Black male graduate students who enter the field of higher education they may struggle with how to enter into the professional world while remaining a student. This constant struggle along with the daily apprehensions of what they may face in the field can possibly cause them to suffer from Racial Battle Fatigue.

The University of Missouri (Mizzou) has experienced its fair share of racial injustices over the last year (Pearson, 2015). While this was a tense time to be a member of the Mizzou community, the media coverage played a large role in the taxation of its minority community. Students, both undergraduate and graduate, banded together in the name of supporting one another through these difficult times (The New York Times, 2015). Creating this informal network of students was a great first step. Groups involved in "The Movement" that were established by Black men and women students was one way they sought to deal with their immediate racial crisis. With the number of Black male graduate students on Mizzou's campus being minimal relative to the institution's size, this was not the only way they were supported.

Various offices and departments on campus as also worked to support Black students while intentionally focusing their efforts on the graduate population. While the Gaines/Oldham Black Culture Center served as a central space of safety and comfort, this was not the only place on campus these students could find support. The University of Missouri Counseling Center provided services that were accessible to the Black males on the campus such as individual and group therapy sessions. The Counseling

Center also created and distributed materials around campus on how to deal with racial trauma.

The Department of Black Studies, Department of Psychological Sciences, and Department of Educational, School, & Counseling Psychology all collaborated on creating a space for students of color to support each other. With the sponsoring departments, they intentionally included their graduate students in their program and campus wide in weekly healing circles to overcome the violence experienced within their communities. With the current high exposure of racism on college campuses, students often feel the need to advocate in various ways. Whether through active protesting, writing of demands, or educating peers on cultural competencies, students of color have been dealing with crisis management while attending universities across the nation. Specifically graduate students of color, who seem to exist on an ambiguous line between "professional" staff member and student must learn coping strategies while remaining strong, yet vigilant, in cases of racial and social unrest. This professional limbo can create apprehension amongst graduate students when they want to express their own concerns and opinions while still serving as a professional resource and advocate for undergraduate students. We want this text to be able to shape and guide dialogue about how institutions of higher learning can better serve and support graduate students in times of crisis, particularly surrounding race relations. We plan to include crisis management strategies and self care techniques that Black male graduate students can adopt as they find the balance between their work, school, and personal lives.

Often times college administrators are models for how to respond to and support students through times of crisis on campus. We must be aware of the impact crisis incidents can have on the diverse student populations we serve. We must be better prepared to address multicultural issues and work effectively with culturally diverse populations and their issues (Reynolds, 2009). This level of attention and effort should not be limited to diverse undergraduate populations; graduate students, particularly those of color, will face the same injustices and crisis as undergraduate students. Student affairs professionals must continue to expand their multicultural competence as it is essential to applying helping behaviors in a higher education context (Reynolds, 2009).

Talbot included that "research has indicated that multicultural training efforts within graduate preparation programs are uneven and often inadequate" (as cited in Reynolds, 2009). With this in mind, student affairs professionals play a crucial role in adequately supporting graduate students of color. In times of racial unrest in the country, college campuses have been largely affected. Many marginalized groups of students may experience several macro and microaggressions that can affect their mental wellness and daily functionality. This is particularly true of Black male graduate students, with the societal villainization of Black men throughout American media (Journal of Blacks in Higher Education, 2016a; Journal of Blacks in Higher Education, 2016b).

Student affairs professional that work directly with graduate students in a supervisory role can be one source of immediate support to assist them through times of crisis. Winston and Cream describe supervision as a "helping process provided by the institutions to benefit or support staff" (as cited in Reynolds, 2009). While graduate students assume the role of paraprofessionals, the student component can be sometimes overlooked. It is imperative for individuals who supervise Black male graduate students, especially during times of racial unrest, to be aware of their multicultural competency. By remaining abreast of multicultural issues, supervisory roles can, in part, assume mentorship roles, allowing for fruitful relationships and outcomes for the graduate student, the supervisor, and the department. However, we cannot continue with the current narrative in the field of education. With these stereotypes and myths about mentoring, student affairs professionals must move towards a functional system of mentoring. Functional mentoring is simply preparing graduate students for careers by promoting visibility and access by the faculty mentor (Thomas et al, 2007). With the increase of racial tensions on college campuses, it can be difficult for graduate students of color to find the social and academic support from faculty members. Thus, the difficult dance of mentor-protégé begins with graduate students of color establishing effective mentoring relationships. In doing so, they will be able to engage with their graduate students in an empathetic manner that allows for validation of the individual's experiences as they work beyond these injustices.

Best Practices

Mentoring is the process by which a novice person (student or mentee) is positively socialized by the sagacious person (faculty or mentor) for the purpose of learning traditions, practices, and framework of a profession, association, or organization (Brown, Davis & McClendon,1999). For this purpose, we as student affairs professionals sees that mentoring can be a vital catalyst for graduate students of color. Thomas, Willis, & Davis (2007) highlights that the success of graduate education depends on a student-faculty relationship based on integrity, trust and support. A true mentoring relationship requires a faculty person to move beyond his or her space as an academic expert to a space of co-discovery (Brown et al, 1999).

Since integration African Americans have faced exclusion from institutions of higher education. Certain stereotypes pertaining to African Americans have limited their academic abilities and competencies as well their unique cultural perspective (Thomas et al, 2007). With these stereotypes and myths about mentoring, student affairs professionals must move towards a functional system of mentoring. Functional mentoring is simply preparing graduate students for careers by promoting visibility and access by the faculty mentor (Thomas et al, 2007). With the increase of racial tensions on college campuses, it can be difficult for graduate students of color to find the social and academic support from faculty members. Thus, the difficult dance of mentor-protégé begins with graduate students of color establishing effective mentoring

relationships.

To understand and construct effective mentoring relationships between mentor and protégé, we must debunk myths surrounding graduate students of color (Brown et al, 1999). The first myth is that engaging with graduate students of color during class and seminars is sufficient mentoring (Brown et al, 1999). Mentoring cannot stop when the class ends or the semester is over, classroom only exchanges does not produce applicable coping methods for out of the classroom interactions. These out-of-class interactions can be the cornerstone of letters of reference for future employment, improvement in self-confidence, and fosters the likelihood that students will enter their selected field (Brown et al, 1999). The second myth is that student of color can only be mentored by faculty of color (Brown et al, 1999). This wrong philosophy continues to have students frequently complaining that they lack mentoring and often have to make their own way through their graduate programs (Thomas et al, 2007). Neglecting the possibility of White faculty members mentoring graduate students of color impedes the possibility Cross-Cultural Mentoring.

Cross-Cultural Mentoring occurs when an individual with different racial/ethnic identities establishes a mentoring relationship (McCoy, Winkle-Wagner & Luedke, 2015). This social exchange allows both mentor and protégé to develop support and appreciation for one another. There are more students of color than faculty of color at many institutions; as such students of color must be mentored by White faculty members (Brown et al, 1999). To equip faculty members, Brown and associates (1999) recommend incorporating diversity and competence training to develop competence among mentors. This training will target conflict management, interpersonal communications and relationship (Brown et al, 1999). Having these vital training sessions limits the lack of trust between graduate students of color and White faculty members. This lack of trust is often a significant barrier in cross-cultural mentoring because of social scripts where people act out their socialized roles (McCoy et al, 2015).

As we have identified mentoring as a possible crisis management technique for graduate students of color, we must convey the benefits. Mentoring provides the protégé with guidance, support, enhanced networking, and feedback regarding career and degree attainment (Thomas et al, 2007). Mentoring graduate students also decrease the possibility of "colorblind" mentoring. Colorblindness is the belief that race should not and does not matter (McCoy et al, 2015). Often White faculty members are likely to engage in "colorblind mentoring" where they attempt to treat all students the same regardless of students backgrounds (McCoy et al, 2015). Mentoring also provides the mentor with reciprocal relationship that allow mentor-protégé shared feelings and values (Thomas et al, 2007). As four brothers currently going through this continuous cycle in academia, it is with great intent that we challenge the narrative of being an educated brother.

Author Biographies

Allison Smith

After spending eight years with the Louisiana Center Addressing Substance Use in Collegiate Communities (LaCASU) as the Associate Director on the campus of Louisiana State University, Dr. Allison M. Smith is currently the Program Administrator for LaCASU at its new home, the Louisiana Board of Regents as of July 2018.

Dr. Smith facilitates the Louisiana Higher Education Coalition (LaHEC), conducts biennial statewide Core Alcohol and Drug Survey administration and provides professional development training around the issue of substance use prevention in Louisiana's colleges. Allison's experience includes internships with both Nurse Family Partnership and the Substance Abuse and Mental Health Services Administration (SAMHSA) in the Center for Substance Abuse Prevention (CSAP).

Dr. Smith, a native of Baton Rouge, Louisiana, received a Bachelor of Science degree in Psychology from Southern University in 2009, a Masters of Public Administration from Louisiana State University in May 2011 followed by a doctoral degree in Educational Leadership, Research and Counseling with a specialization in Higher Education Administration in 2016 also from Louisiana State University. You can contact Dr. Smith at www.drallisonmichellesmith.com.

Anthony Walker

Dr. Anthony Walker currently serves as the Assistant Director of Academic Initiatives at Tarrant County College where he serves on the leadership team for the College's Guided Pathways model planning and coordinates the day-to-day responsibilities for the Carl D. Perkins Basic Grant project.

For more than a decade, Anthony has focused on integrating principles of inclusiveness in action and identity development into his career as a scholar-practitioner. Having had the opportunity to serve in entry, mid-level, and executive leadership roles, Dr. Walker has a diverse set of experiences in educational practice. However, amid the diversity in settings and positions, using education to promote values of social justice, equity-mindedness, and inquiry have remained central tenets of his work. His research interests include topics such as: intersections of difference, identity development, systems of privilege, and curriculum development.

Originally from Maysville, Kentucky, Anthony earned his Bachelor of Arts in Elementary Education from Northern Kentucky University, his Master of Education in Educational Counseling from Texas Christian University, and his Doctor of Education in Educational Leadership from Stephen F. Austin State University.

Brandon Jamaal Stroud

Brandon Jamaal Stroud, a native of Fountain Inn, South Carolina, studied at the University of South Carolina Upstate where he obtained a B.S. in Interdisciplinary Studies. His journey led him to the Warner Graduate School of Education and Human Development at the University of Rochester where he received an M.S. in Higher Education - Student Affairs. Brandon is employed at the Rochester Institute of Technology in the Center of Residence Life as a Residential Coordinator. He serves on a research team that focuses on urban neighborhood development, civil engagement, and educational reform in the local Rochester community. This project focuses on creating general hubs in the community that offers a transformation for community and mind. His doctoral research focuses on the transformation of access to education as it relates to the history of African Americans.

Donald Gilliam

Donald Gilliam is a student support specialist at University of Missouri, having spent more than 10 years at the university as an undergraduate, graduate, and professional staff member.

Jazzmine Brooks

Jazzmine Brooks is the Violence Prevention and Green Dot Coordinator in Student Wellness at Iowa State University. Brooks coordinates the development, education and oversight of staff and students relating to violence prevention efforts on and off campus. Brooks is a native to Chicago, Illinois, however calls Las Vegas, Nevada home. Brooks is an advocate for social change, and believes in creating space to discuss and resolve social justice issues. She is a member of the Zeta Phi Beta Sorority, Incorporated.

Joshua Fredenburg

Dr. Joshua Fredenburg is a Nationally Acclaimed Speaker, Author of Five Books, Tedx Speaker, and President/Founder of the 'Award Winning Circle of Change Leadership Experience that specializes in helping student leaders discover the leader from within, develop skills to serve and lead diverse groups of people effectively, and the inspiration and courage to become a leader that makes a positive impact. For the past fourteen years, Joshua has not only served as a keynote speaker in 47 states across the nation, but he has transformed the lives of thousands of people as a keynote speaker, workshop presenter, trainer, and facilitator at different conferences, retreats, training, graduations, and events.

In addition to a successful speaking career, Joshua obtained a Master's Degree in Organizational Leadership from Biola University in 2008; received his Doctoral Degree in Organizational Leadership from Nova Southeastern University in June of 2019, has appeared on various television/radio shows, and is the leader and founder of a leadership movement that impacts student leaders each year in Los Angeles, California and New York City, and has reached a total of 1,700 plus student leaders from more 100 universities and colleges over the past nine years.

Khristian Kemp-Delisser

A lifelong social justice educator, they have worked in Residence Life, LGBT Student Services, and Multicultural Affairs at various public and private universities, including the University of Illinois, Urbana Champaign; University of Vermont; and Colgate University. They have researched and presented widely at regional and national conferences on the experiences, needs, and cultural practices of LGBTQ+ students and staff of color in higher education. Inside the classroom, they have designed and taught courses on creative writing, gender and sexuality, student development theory, and intergroup dialogue.

They have served on non-profit boards, consulted with high schools, businesses, and educational organizations that serve LGBTQ+ youth and adults, including Outright VT, Pride Center of VT, and Central New York Alliance of LGBTQ Offices and Resources. They hold a Bachelors degree from Syracuse University, and a Masters and Ed.D, both from the University of Vermont.

Kemp-Delisser is owner and CEO of Out Loud Dialogues LLC, an educational consulting firm that provides a variety of services, resources and tools to facilitate inter- and intra-group dialogue. Contact outloudialogues@gmail.com for information about our services, including proofreading and editing services, live or virtual presentations, webinars, keynote speeches, training and facilitation.

LaToya Rene Robertson

LaToya Rene Robertson is a well versed student affairs pro. Like Many she began as an RA, later as a professional has served as Director of First Year Experience, Resident Director, adjunct faculty, and Service Learning Fellowship recipient. LaToya René Is an author of "The College Cheat Sheet" released in 2016 and, contributing author of "Speaking From Within" which is set to release March 2019. LaToya René can be found speaking when she is not working directly with students. Most notable presentations are her presentation at Hawaii International Conference on Education and her TED Talk "Vision = Victory." Robertson is in the the final stages of her Ph.D in Educational Leadership and Policy Students. For more information please visit LaToyaRene.com or contact her at lr@latoyarene.com

Lyndsey Williams Mayweather

Lyndsey Williams Mayweather currently serves as the Assistant Director for Student Life and Engagement at Augusta University in Augusta, GA directly overseeing the areas of Orientation, Parent and Family Programs, Greek Life, and Graduate Student Government. Previously Lyndsey worked at a large state institution in the midwest where she met Jazzmine. Lyndsey received her Bachelor's of Science degree in Psychology with a minor in Health Science from Clemson University in Clemson, South Carolina and a Master's of Science degree in Higher Education with an emphasis in Student Affairs from The Florida State University. Lyndsey is a Doctoral student at the University of Georgia studying Learning, Leadership, and Organizational Development.

Marcellus Braxton

Marcellus has a bachelor's degree in Political Science, Philosophy, and Economics with an African Studies Certificate from the University of Pittsburgh along with an M.A. in Philosophy from the University of Missouri, and a Juris Doctor (J.D) from the University of North Carolina School of Law. He is currently the Director of the African American Cultural Center at Austin Peay State University, and he works on issues of race, diversity, social justice, equity, and inclusion for the University. He has also previously worked at Missouri S&T as a Coordinator for the Student Diversity, Outreach, and Women's Programs. Additionally, he teaches courses in Political Science, African American Studies, and the First Year Experience at Austin Peay State University.

Michael J. Seaberry

Michael J. Seaberry is a poet, educator, motivational speaker, entrepreneur, and activist. He is a doctoral student at Louisiana State University with work centering on racism in education and battling racial injustices such as the school-to prison pipeline, student activism on predominately white campuses, and healing during times of racial unrest. His publications include articles in The Journal of Critical Scholarship on Higher Education and Student Affairs, Diverse: Issues in Higher Education, and books chapters with Lexington Press. Michael is also the Founder/CEO of Fearless Flying, a new age motivating and educational consulting firm. He has also published his first book, "The Mississippi Crying: A Collection of Poems, Stories of Healing" which is available on Amazon. Michael lives in Baton Rouge, Louisiana and can be reached at FearlessFlyingMJS@gmail.com.

Michael R. Williams

Michael is an excellent decision maker and holds many sterling qualities. He is collegial with colleagues and empathic to needs of students at our university. He has an ability to fit in with the dynamics of a wide range of groups. He is a consummate professional in all of his dealings with students, faculty, and senior level administrators. He pushes students beyond their boundaries to seek true learning and understanding of the world around them. He constantly seeks new and creative approaches to educate students through his innovative programming through our cultural center. He has the ability to work well under deadline pressures and connect with diverse groups of students. He embraces diversity in all forms and this contributes to his being a fantastic cultural center director.

Patience D. Bryant

Dr. Patience D. Bryant is the Director for Student Conduct and Ethical Development at California State University at Long Beach, where she is overseeing the creation and implementation of the university's first restorative justice program: W.A.V.E. (Welcoming Accountable Voices & Education).

Dr. Bryant holds a Ph.D. in Conflict Analysis and Resolution from Nova Southeastern University. She formerly served as the Associate Director for Campus Life & Student Development at Texas A&M University Commerce and as the first Student Conduct Coordinator for the Department of Student Housing at the University of Mississippi, where she also restorative justice into their current student conduct programs. Dr. Bryant serves as a faculty member for the Donald D. Gehring Academy by the Association for Student Conduct Administrators (ASCA) and serves at the Director of Education for the ASCA Board of Directors.

Patricia Tita Feraud-King

Patricia "Tita" Feraud-King is currently a full-time Higher Education doctoral student at the University of Massachusetts-Amherst and works in Residence Education. She is also an active member in Graduate Employee Organization union. Her research interests are centered on higher education's lack of inclusion and access for students of color, staff of color, first-generation students, and low-income students and the intersection of the marginalized identities. Mx. Feraud-King is currently conducting inquiries on the experiences of first and second-generation Africana immigrants at historically white institutions.

As a Massachusetts native, she graduated from the College of the Holy Cross with a Bachelor of Arts in Sociology and a concentration in Peace and Conflict Studies. Mx. Feraud-King also obtained her Master's of Science in Higher Education from the University of Pennsylvania.

Mx. Feraud-King is known for her passion and expertise on social justice-related work. Some of her past workshops and presentations were on topics as environmental justice, ways one can engage in courageous conversations, and the feminist identity at a residential college in Australia. Mrs. Feraud-King accumulated ten years of experience in facilitation, public speaking (including being a conference's keynote speaker), and community organizing.

Prentiss A. Dantzler

Prentiss Dantzler is an Assistant Professor in the Urban Studies Institute. Currently, Prentiss' research is focused on four projects: 1) housing and transportation expenditures across urban form types, 2) the role of nonprofit organizations in shaping gentrification narratives, 3) the role of homeowners associations in maintaining segregation patterns, and 4) racial capitalism and urban development processes.

Prentiss' research has appeared in a number of academic journals including *Housing Studies*, *Urban Affairs Review* and *Research in Social Movements, Conflict and Change*. He also serves on the Editorial Board for *City and Community*. Prentiss has written for popular media outlets including *Blackademia*, *Shelterforce*, *The Conversation*, and *The Huffington Post*. In 2017, Prentiss received the 40 for 40 Fellowship from the Association for Public Policy Analysis & Management for his early career contribution to the field of public policy. Prior to joining the Urban Studies Institute, Prentiss was an Assistant Professor of Sociology and Mellon Faculty Fellow at Colorado College. In the Fall of 2019, he was in residence in the Department of Sociology at the University of Toronto as a U.S. Fulbright Scholar.

Tish Norman

Tish Norman is a well-known, highly regarded professional speaker, which is why her keynotes have become favorites among organizations, universities, and leadership conferences from coast to coast. She is venerated for delivering tailored, measurable training solutions for corporate, government, and non-profit organizations of all sizes and challenges her audiences to actively contribute to the transformation and growth of their organizations.

Tish is a contributing author of two books: *Leading the Way: Stories of Inspiration and Leadership* and *From Mediocre to Magnificent: How to Make the Rest of Your Life the Best of Your Life.* Additionally, she's written several articles featured in higher education magazines and was a finalist in *Campus Activities Magazine*'s Speaker of the Year.

Tish is a graduate of Kentucky State University, has a Master of Arts in Education from Pepperdine University and is currently a PhD pursuant in Pan-African Studies, where her research focuses on memory & the experiences of the contemporary Black sorority. Having spoken in 45 states and 14 countries and despite her rigorous academic obligations,

Tish still maintains an active speaking schedule, keynoting at dozens of leadership conferences and campuses every year. For bookings, email Tish@TishNorman.com IG @iamtishnorman / FB @tishnorman / Twitter @tishnorman / www.TishNorman.com

Tracy N. Stokes

An educator for over 15 years, Tracy McMillan Stokes, M.Ed. has served as an academic advisor, college access manager, and diversity/inclusion educator. Her passion to empower her clients to live "on purpose" is evident as she works to create programming, events, and business solutions that assist them with realizing and achieving their dreams. An entrepreneur at heart, she is the founder of 3 brands (TraSpeaks, LLC, the MTSS Collective, and Young P.E.A.R.L.S., Inc.) that assists individuals, especially women, activate their voice in purpose through workshops, customized coaching sessions, and educational programming.

Originally from Dayton, Ohio she holds a Bachelor of Arts Degree in Sociology and Master of Education in Higher Education Administration from Wright State University. An active member of the Cincinnati/ Northern Kentucky region, she is a graduate of Leadership Northern Kentucky Class of 2015, a past participant in the Higher Education Collaborative of Greater Cincinnati's Women's Institute for Leadership Development, a member of the NKY Branch of the NAACP, and is a member of Alpha Kappa Alpha Sorority, Inc. She is the proud mother of young adult, Alexis and teenagers, Miles and Justin. You can connect with me on my website www.tracynicole.org and via email tracy@tracynicole.org

Zachary E. Shirley

Dr. Zachary E. Shirley currently serves as the Assistant Dean for Sorority and Fraternity Life at Indiana University Bloomington, where he oversees the staffing, budgetary, and programmatic efforts for both leadership and inclusion initiatives within the office of Student Life & Learning.

Originally from Dallas, Texas, Dr. Shirley graduated with his Bachelor of Science Degree in Secondary Education/English from Paul Quinn College (2005), his Master of Science in Higher Education Administration from Texas A&M University-Commerce (2006), and his Doctor of Education Degree from the University of North Texas (2014), with his dissertation research centered on the perceptions of Fraternities and Sororities from the perspective of a single institution and its community.

Dr. Shirley has worked as a Student Affairs professional for more than ten years, with previous experiences from Texas Woman's University, the University of Texas at Dallas, Texas A&M University-Commerce, and the University of Cincinnati in areas such as Fraternity & Sorority Life, Student Activities, Orientation, Student Government, Volunteer Services, and Mentorship Programs. Dr. Shirley's personal philosophy in regards to working with students is to inspire the students, so that they may, in turn, impact the world.

References

Chapter 1 - Authenticity Challenges within the Workplace for African American Student Affairs Professionals

When You Are Needed, But Not Wanted!

NAMI. (n.d.). African American Mental Health. Retrieved from www.nami.org/Find-Support/Diverse-Communities/African-Americans

Sue, D. W. (2010). Racial Microaggressions in Everyday Life. Retrieved from www.psychologytoday.com/blog/microaggressions-in-everyday-life/201010/racial-microaggressions-in-everyday-life

Williams, M. T. (2015). The Link Between Racism and PTSD. Retrieved from www.psychologytoday.com/blog/culturally-speaking/201509/the-link-between-racism-and-ptsd

Showing Up: Owning the Everyday Struggle of Authenticity at PWIs

Duncan, P. (2014). Hot Commodities, Cheap Labor: Women of color in the academy. *Frontiers: A Journal of Women Studies 35*(3), 39-63. University of Nebraska Press.

Thomas, G. D. and Hollenshead, C. (2001). Resisting from the Margins: The coping strategies of Black women and other women of color faculty members at a research university. *The Journal of Negro Education, 70*(3), 166-175.

Chapter 2 – Cultural Competence Challenges of African American Student Affairs Professionals

The Struggle is Real: Becoming a More Informed, Inclusive, and Intersectional Advisor of Black Greek-Letter Organizations

Astin, A. W. (1993). Diversity and multiculturalism on the campus: How are students affected? Change: The Magazine of Higher Learning, 25(2), 44-49.

Crenshaw, K. (1989). Demarginalizing the intersection of race and sex: A black feminist critique of antidiscrimination doctrine, feminist theory and antiracist politics. U. Chi. Legal F., 139.

Giddings, P. (1988). In search of sisterhood: The history of Delta Sigma Theta Sorority. Inc. New York: Morrow.

Harper, S.R. (2000, Fall). The academic standings report: Helping NPHC chapters make the grade. Association of Fraternity Advisors Perspectives, 14-17.

Harper, S. (2008). The effects of sorority and fraternity membership on class participation and African American student engagement in predominantly White classroom environments. College Student Affairs Journal, 27(1), 94-115.

Kimbrough, W. M. (2003). Black Greek 101: The culture, customs, and challenges of Black fraternities and sororities. Fairleigh Dickinson Univ Press.

Kimbrough, W. M., &; Hutcheson, P. A. (1998). The impact of membership in Black Greek-letter organizations on Black students, involvement in collegiate activities and their development of leadership skills. Journal of Negro Education, 96-105.

McClure, S. M. (2006). Improvising masculinity: African American fraternity membership in the construction of a Black masculinity. Journal of African American Studies, 10(1), 57-73.

Mitchell, D., Jr., Weathers, J. D., & Jones, M. A. (2013). A 20-year history of Black Greek-letter organization research and scholarship. Bloomington, IN: Indiana University

Parker, M. H. (1990). Alpha Kappa Alpha Through the Years, 1908-1988. Mobium Press.

Pascarella, E., Edison, M., Whitt, E. J., Nora, A., Hagedorn, L. S., & Terenzini, P. (1996). Cognitive effects of Greek affiliation during the first year of college. NASPA Journal, 33(4), 242-259.

Patton, L. D., Bridges, B. K, & Flowers, L. A. (2011). Effects of Greek affiliation on African American students; engagement: differences by college racial composition. College Student Affairs Journal, 2 29: 113-123.

Ross, L. C. (2000). The divine nine: The history of African American fraternities and sororities. Kensington Books.

Strayhorn, T. L., & McCall, F. C. (2012). Cultural competency of Black Greek-letter organization advisors. Journal of African American Studies, 16(4), 700-715.

Chapter 3 – Racial Battle Fatigue Challenges for African American Student Affairs Professionals

FUBU: The Necessity of Organic Safe Spaces for Black Women Higher Education Administrators, Created For Us, By Us.

Blackwood, J. & Brown-Welty, S. (2011). Chapter 6 Mentoring and interim positions: Pathways to leadership for women of color. In G. Jean-Marie, B. Lloyd-Jones (Eds.), *Women of color in higher education: Changing directions and new perspectives* (pp. 109-133). Retrieved from http://dx.doi.org/10.1108/S1479-3644-(2011)0000010010

Collins, P.H. (1986). Learning from the outsider within: The sociological significance of Black feminist thought. *Social Problems*, 33(6), 14-32.

Collins, P.H. (1998). It's all in the family: Intersections of gender, race and nation. *Hypatia*,13(3), 62-82.

Collins, P.H. (2000). Black feminist thought: Knowledge, consciousness, and the politics of empowerment (Perspectives on gender). Taylor and Francis. Kindle Edition.

Crenshaw, K. (1989). Demarginalizing the intersection of race and sex: A Black feminist critique of antidiscrimination doctrine, feminist theory and antiracist politics. *The University of Chicago Legal Forum*, 139-167.

Dawkins, L.S. (2012). Historically Black college or university or predominantly white institution? Choosing your institutional path. In Jones, T. B., Dawkins, L. S., McClinton, M. M., & Glover, M. H. (Eds.), *Pathways to Higher Education Administration for African American Women* (pp. 4 – 17). Sterling, VA: Stylus Publishing.

Eriksson, M., Dahlgren, L., Janlert, U., Weinehall, L., & Emmelin, M. (2010). Social capital, gender and educational level: impact on self-rated health. *The Open Public Health Journal, 3*, 1-12.

Glover, M. H. (2012). Existing pathways: A historical overview of Black women in higher education administration. In Jones, T. B., Dawkins, L. S., McClinton, M. M., & Glover, M. H. (Eds.), *Pathways to Higher Education Administration*

for African American Women (pp. 4-17).
Sterling, VA: Stylus Publishing.

Guillory, R.M. (2001). Strategies for overcoming the barriers of being an African-American administrator on a predominantly White university campus. In Jones, L. (Ed.), *Retaining African Americans in higher education: Challenging paradigms for retaining students, faculty, and administrators.* (pp. 111-123). Sterling, VA: Stylus Publishing.

hooks, b. (1984). Feminist theory: From margin to center. Boston: South End Press.

Howard-Hamilton, M. & Patitu, C.L. (2012). Decisions to make or not make along the career path. In Jones, T. B., Dawkins, L. S., McClinton, M. M., & Glover, M. H. (Eds.), *Pathways to Higher Education Administration for African American Women* (pp. 85-102). Sterling, VA: Stylus Publishing.

Intersection of race and gender in workspace silos at Predominantly White Institutions (Doctoral dissertation). Retrieved from LSU Doctoral Dissertations. (3470).

Jackson, J. F. L. (2001). A new test for diversity: Retaining African-American administrators at Predominantly White Institutions. In Jones, L. (Ed.), *Retaining African Americans in higher education: Challenging paradigms for retaining students, faculty, and administrators.* (pp. 93-109). Sterling, VA: Stylus Publishing.

Jones, T. B. & Dufor, W. (2012). Direction along the path: Mentoring and Black female administrators. In Jones, T. B., Dawkins, L. S., McClinton, M. M., & Glover, M. H. (Eds.), *Pathways to Higher Education Administration for African American Women* (pp. 27-36). Sterling, VA: Stylus Publishing.

King, J., & Gomez, G.G. (2008). On the pathway to the presidency: Characteristics of higher education's senior leaders. Washington, DC: American Council on Education.

McCray, E. (2011). Chapter 5 woman(ist)s' work: The experiences of Black women scholars in education at predominantly white institutions. In Frierson, H. T. (Series Ed.), *Diversity in Higher Education: Vol. 9. Women of color in higher education: Feminist theoretical perspectives* (pp. 99-125). http://dx.doi.org/10.1108/S1479-3644(2011)0000009010

Mercer, S. H., Ziegler-Hill, V., Wallace, M., & Hayes, D. M. (2011). Development and initial validation of the Inventory of Microaggressions Against Black Individuals. *Journal of Counseling Psychology*, 58(4), 457-469.

Rosette, A. S. & Livingston, R. (2012). Failure is not an option for Black women: Effects of organizational performance on leaders with single versus dual-subordinate identities. *Journal of Experimental Social Psychology*, 48, pp. 1162-1167.

Sellers, R. M., Smith, M.A., Shelton, J. N., Rowley, S. A. J., & Chavous, T. M. (1998). Multidimensional Model of Racial Identity: A reconceptualization of African American racial identity. *Personality and Social Psychology Review*, 2 (1), pp. 18-39.

Smith, A.M. (2016). Black girl magic: How Black women administrators navigate the

Smith, W. A., Allen, W. R., & Danley, L. L. (2007). "Assume the position … you fit the description": Psychosocial experiences and racial battle fatigue among African American male college students. American Behavioral Scientist, 51(4), pp. 551-578. doi: 10.1177/0002764207307742

Sue, D. W., Capodilupo, C. M., Torino, G. C., Bucceri, J. M., Holder, A., Nadal, K. L., & Esquilin, M. (2007). Racial microaggressions in everyday life: implications for clinical practice. *American psychologist, 62*(4), 271-286.

Verde, L. A. (2011). Chapter 3 women of color: Their path to leadership makes for a better higher education for all. In Frierson, H. T. (Series Ed.), Diversity in Higher Education: Vol. 9. Women of color in higher education: Turbulent past, promising future. (pp. 49-75). doi: 10.1108/S1479-3644(2011)0000009008

Interrupting The Narrative: Racial Battle Fatigue

Dugas, M. J., Gagnon, F., Ladouceur, R., & Freeston, M. H. (1998). Generalized anxiety disorder: A preliminary test of a conceptual model. Behaviour Research and Therapy, 36(2), 215-226. Retrieved from http://dx.doi.org/10.1016/S0005-7967(97)00070-3

Smith, W. A., Allen, W. R., & Danley, L. L. (2007). "Assume the position ... you fit the description": Psychosocial experiences and racial battle fatigue among African American male college students. American Behavioral Scientist, 51(4), pp. 551-578. doi: 10.1177/0002764207307742

Sue, D. W. (2010). Racial Microaggressions in Everyday Life. Retrieved from www.psychologytoday.com/blog/microaggressions-in-everyday-life/201010/racial-microaggressions-in-everyday-life

Chapter 4 – Intersectionality Challenges for African American Student Affairs Professionals

Developing Expertise Beyond Our Professional Roles: Discussing Race & Privilege Within Higher Education

Lorde, A. (1984.) Sister Outsider : Essays and Speeches. Trumansburg, NY :Crossing Press.

Michaels, W. B. (2007). The Trouble with Diversity: How We Learned to Love Identity and Ignore Inequality New York, Owl.

Palca, J. (2015). A Discoverer of the Buckyball Offers Tips On Winning A Nobel Prize. National Public Radio. Retrieved from: https://www.npr.org/2015/10/08/445339243/a-discoverer-of-the-buckyball-offers-tips-on-winning-a-nobel-prize

Gay & Queer Black Men in Student Affairs

Battle, J., Cohen, C., Warren, D., Fergerson, G., and Audam, S. (2002). Say It Loud: I'm Black and I'm Proud; Black Pride Survey 2000. New York: The Policy Institute of the National LGBTQ Task Force.

Bryant, L. Isaac-Savage, E.P., & Bowman, L. (2014). Reflections on the Spirituality of Three Black Gay Men. In Proceedings of the Adult Education Research Conference. Retrieved from http://www.adulterc.org/Proceedings/2014/papers/Bryant.pdf

Dilley, P. (2005). Which way out? A typology of nonheterosexual male collegiate identities. Journal of Higher Education, 76, 56-88.

Harper, S. R. (2012). *Black male student success in higher education: A report from the National*

Black Male College Achievement Study.
Philadelphia: University of Pennsylvania,
Center for the Study of Race and Equity in
Education.

Johnson III, R.G. (2017). Leadership and Racing
Toward the Arc of Freedom by African
American Gay and Bisexual Men. In Mitchell,
P. (Ed)., *African American Males in Higher
Education Leadership: Challenges and
Opportunities*. New York, NY: Peter Lang
Press.

kemp-delisser, k. (2015). My anger is never gonna
mellow: Campus climate & queer students of
color. In Aiken, J., Flash, L., Heading-Grant,
W., and Miller, F. (Eds.), *Theory to practice:
Fostering diverse and inclusive campus
environments.* NCPEA Press

kemp-delisser, k. & Higgins, J. (2016, March). *LGB
Students of Color and Cultural Capital.*
Workshop presented at the National
Association of Student Personnel
Administrators Annual Conference,
Indianapolis, IN.

Means, D.R., & Jaeger, A.J. (2013). Black in the
rainbow: "Quaring" the Black gay male student
experience at historically Black universities.
*Journal of African American Males in
Education*, 4(2), 124-140.

Mumford, K. (2016). *Not Straight, Not White: Black
Gay Men from the March on Washington to the
AIDS Crisis*. Durham, NC: University of North
Carolina Press.

Poynter, K. & Washington, J. (2005). Multiple
identities: Creating community on campus for
LGBT students. In S. R. Rankin. *Campus
climate for sexual minorities*. New Directions
for Student Services, no. 111. pp. 41-47. San
Francisco: Jossey-Bass.

Strayhorn, T.L., Johnson, R.M., Henderson, T.S., & Tillman-Kelly, D.L. (2015). *Beyond coming out: New insights about GLBQ college students of color.* Columbus, OH: Center for Higher Education Enterprise, The Ohio State University.

Strayhorn, T., & Tillman-Kelly, D. (2013). Queering Masculinity: Manhood and Black Gay Men in College. *Spectrum: A Journal on Black Men, 1*(2), 83-110.

Wozolek, B., Varndell, R., & Speer, T. (2015). Are we not fatigued? Queer battle fatigue at the intersection of heteronormative culture. International Journal of Curriculum and Social Justice, 1(1), 186-214.

Chapter 5 – Institutionalized Racism Challenges for African American Student Affairs Professionals

Personal Storytelling: A Tool to Counter Institutional Racism

Alexander, B. K. (2008). Performance ethnography: The reenacting and inciting of culture. In N.K. Denzin, & Y. S. Lincoln (Eds.), Strategies of qualitative inquiry (3 rd ed., pp. 75-112). Thousand Oaks, CA: Sage Publications, Inc.

ASHE (2013). Diverse student identity and capacity development. ASHE Higher Education Report, 39(4), 29-54.

ASHE (2005). Organizing for Diversity: Fundamental issues. ASHE Higher Education Report, 31(1), 49-61.

ASHE (2002). Integration of identity development theory into practice. ASHE Higher Education Report, 29(6), 79-99.

Bell, L. A., Castañeda, C., & Zuñiga, X. (2010). Racism: Introduction. In M. Adams, W.

J.Blumenfield, C. Castañeda, H. W. Hackman, M. L. Peters, & X. Zuñiga (Eds.), Reading for diversity and social justice (2 nd ed.), (pp. 59-66). New York, NY: Routledge.

Bess, J.L., & Dee, J.R. (2008). Understanding college and university organization: Theories for effective policy and practice (Vol. 1). Sterling, VA: Stylus Publications.

Chambers, T. C. (2005). The special role of higher education in society: As a public good for the public good. In A. J. Kezar, T. C. Chambers, J. C. Burkhardt, & Associates (Eds.), Higher education for the public good: Emerging voices from a national movement, (pp.3-22). San Francisco, CA: Josey-Bass.

Cho, S., Crenshaw, K. W., & L. McCall. (2013). Toward a field of intersectionality studies:Theory, applications, and praxis. Signs: Journal of Women in Culture and Society, 38(4), 785-810.

Clandinin, D. J., & Connelly, F. M. (2000). Narrative inquiry: Experience and story in qualitative research. San Francisco, CA: Josey Wiley & Sons, Inc.

Creswell, J. W. (2009). Research design: Qualitative, quantitative, and mixed methods approaches (3rd ed.). Thousand Oaks, CA: Sage Publications

Green, D. O., & Trent, W. T. (2005). The public good and a racially diverse democracy. In A. J.Kezar, T. C. Chambers, J. C. Burkhardt, & Associates (Eds.), Higher education for the public good: Emerging voices from a national movement, (pp. 102-123). San Francisco, CA: Josey-Bass.

Jones, R.A. (2005). Race and revisability. Journal of Black Studies, 35: 612–632.

Omi, M., & Winant, H. (2009). Racial formations. In A. Ferber, C. M. Jimenez, A. O. Herrera, D. R.

Samuels (Eds.), The matrix reader: Examining the dynamics of oppression and privilege (pp. 51-57). New York, NY: McGraw-Hill Companies, Inc.

Scott, O. (ed.) (1997). Lines, borders and connections: Challenges and possibilities in Multicultural America. Dubuque, Iowa: Kendall/Hunt Publishing.

Sussman, R. W. (2014). The myth: The troubling persistence of an unscientific idea of race. Cambridge, MA: Harvard University Press.

Wachtel, P. L. (1999). Race in the mind of America: Breaking the vicious circle between blacks and whites. New York, NY: Routledge.

Chapter 6 –Microaggressions, Macroaggressions, Stereotypes, and Biases: Challenges for African American Student Affairs Professionals

For Brothers: Developmental Struggles of Black Male Graduate Students

Brown II, C. M., Davis, G. L., & McClendon, S. A. (1999). Mentoring Graduate Students of Color: Myths, Models, and Modes. *Peabody Journal of Education, 74*(2), 105-118.

Journal of Blacks in Higher Education. (2016a). *Study ranks colleges where Twitter use is most derogatory towards blacks.* Retrieved from from https://www.jbhe.com/2016/05/study-ranks-colleges-where-twitter-use-is-the-most-derogatory-to ward-blacks/

Journal of Blacks in Higher Education. (2016b). *Image of President Obama in a noose appears on board members' webpage.* Retrieved from https://www.jbhe.com/2016/07/image-of-president-obama-in-a-noose-appears-on-board-members-web-page/

McCoy, D. L., Winkle-Wagner, R., & Kuedke, C. L. (2015). Colorblind mentoring? Exploring white faculty mentoring of students of color. *Journal of Diversity in Higher Education*, 8(4), 225-242. doi:10.1037/a0038676

The New York Times. (2015). Racial tension and protests on campuses across the country. Retrieved from http://www.nytimes.com/2015/11/11/us/racial-tension-and-protests-on-campuses-across-the-country.html?_r=1

Pearson, M. (2015). A timeline of the University of Missouri protests. CNN. Retrieved from http://www.cnn.com/2015/11/09/us/missouri-protest-timeline/

Reynolds, A. L. (2009). Helping college students: Developing essential support skills for student affairs practice. San Francisco, CA: Jossey-Bass.

Thomas, K. M., Willis, L. A., & Davis, J. (2007). Mentoring minority graduate students: Issues and strategies for institutions, faculty, and students. Equal Opportunities International, 26 (3), 178-192.

Made in the USA
Middletown, DE
17 February 2020